In Search of
Death

In Search of the Death-Less State

And The Many Benefits To Be Had Along The Way

Eric Dowsett

Copyright © 2024 by Eric Dowsett.

All rights reserved.

No portion of this book may be reproduced—mechanically, electronically, or by any other means, including photocopying—without the express written permission of the author.

ISBN-13: 978-0-6482706-1-4
Ebook: 978-0-6482706-2-1

First Printing

Cover designed by Steffi Schott
Typeset and designed by Patricia Wallenburg
Edited by Judy Duguid

Contents

Introduction: Our Journey ix
To Begin 1
Clearing: An Introduction 5
The Shadow 9
Our Journey 13
The Mind 17
The Nervous System Accessing The Mind 21
What Do You Believe? 27
But What Is a Point of View? 31
A Computer Simulation? 33
Oh if It Were So Simple 37
Truly a Dilemma 41
Accessing a Bigger Picture 45
Where Your Attention Goes 47
The Bardos 49
A Challenging Concept 53
Clearing and the Practice of Acceptance 55
And of Course Nothing Really Changes 57
Obscurations 63

Unfinished Business 75

Collapsing Our Shadow. 81

So What Was It Gautama Siddhartha Was Looking For? 83

The Web of Indra 85

Is This the Definition of Madness? 89

Full Circle 93

Heaven and Hell 95

Life Is a Continuing Unfolding 105

Stop Running Away 119

Warning! You Are Approaching the Death-Less State 135

To Summarise the Death-Less State 139

About the Author 145

The many benefits to be experienced along the way . . .

Introduction: Our Journey

*A journey into understanding our life,
our journey from a different perspective.*

Before I begin, I want to be sure that you, the reader, understand this is my story, my journey. It may or may not reflect yours; it may or may not make any sense to you. Above all, I make no definitive claims as to how things are. This is my experience seen through the eyes of my journey.

The Buddha was reported to have begun each of his sermons with the words *'Thus have I heard,'* thereby making no claim to any truth. I do the same.

I will often refer to the teachings of the Buddha; yet I have had almost no formal training in Buddhism. I have read a lot and been interested in these teachings for many years but have not studied with any teacher. My understandings of the teaching, as I share in this book, are based on personal realisations that have arisen as a result of my following the practice of 'Clearing'.

'Clearing', for the uninitiated, is a practice of acceptance. Acceptance beginning with various feelings that we notice in the body. When we first practice Clearing, we believe that we are Clearing another. When we open ourselves up to noticing change in the body which appears to be the result of 'connecting' to another, we first start to realise that when our attention goes to another and change happens, physiologically, in the body, that this 'feeling' arises as a result of this connection to another. This helps us become more objective about the feeling, which in turn helps us to not take it personally.

We learn to not judge the feeling, attach no blame to the feeling and above all not take that particular feeling personally. As we stop giving energy to the feeling, it quickly passes through the body. With enough practice our body gets used to a much broader range of feelings; it begins to feel safe with all these feelings and eventually, with enough practice, is able to simply acknowledge all feelings yet identifying with none.

This may leave you with the impression that you have become a zombie. This is not the case of course. What it does mean is that you are able to experience a broad range of emotions without getting lost in any of them. This will equate to an open, fearless, compassionate heart, no longer a victim to past conditioning.

The many benefits of this way of being are, for the most part, difficult to truly comprehend without walking the path and finding out for yourself what a life lived without being controlled by old, subconscious conditioning is like.

Having said that, I have been on this path for many years and have accepted and embraced an incredibly wide range of emotions and feelings. Just how this has affected my views on life, my perceptions and beliefs, will be explained later in the book.

There will be many points made in this book that will be repeated, often several times. Many times they will be explored from a slightly different angle. There is a reason for this repetition. When any new concept is presented to us, it may not be easily accepted or assimilated. Repetition just reinforces new ways of being, allowing them to be more easily accepted and understood.

To Begin

Thus have I heard/read/experienced.

To even begin to understand why anyone would want to experience the Death-Less State requires that we understand a little of the journey of Gautama Siddhartha, later to become known as the Buddha, the Enlightened One.

My memory of much of this may not be as accurate as some; I make no claims to accuracy, just share as I remember. (Apologies to other students of Buddhism. They may well understand things differently. Here I write for the layperson who may have had no exposure to these teachings.)

It was projected, before Gautama was born into a royal family, that he would be a leader of men. His father, the king, wanted to protect him from this future, so he built a palace with great walls. The little prince, Gautama, was kept safely within these walls, hidden from life outside the palace.

Having grown into a young man, married with a son, he must have been curious—'What was on the other side of the palace wall.' He would have heard the sounds of the world outside, so one day he decided to see for himself. Disguised, with a friend, he left the palace. It must have been quite a shock, for the world outside was nothing like the world inside the palace.

Inside the palace, life was comfortable, all the good things in life were his to command; yet outside he witnessed old age, sickness and death, things he had been shielded from. Unsettled by this, by opening his eyes to a different reality, this young prince wanted to understand what was happening and seek a way beyond the suffering he saw amongst the people.

After returning to the palace, he could not settle back into his life of luxury and decided to leave the palace to learn more, to better understand this process of life, ageing and death.

Thus began a journey that would ultimately lead to his enlightened state, or as the title of this book suggests, the Death-Less State.

Simply put, our young prince first followed other ascetics who claimed to be looking for the same thing. This was a simple life, a life of denial of pleasures and comfortable living. According to the stories, he tried many of these paths, eventually going to the extremes of self-denial. He must have realised that no one on this path had achieved this Death-Less State and so denounced it and returned to a more comfortable life. But this 'comfortable' life offered no answers or true understanding either, which led him to what is now known in Buddhism as the middle way.

This determination had him sitting in meditation, determined not to move until he had reached an enlightened state. And so after being in a deep meditative state for quite some time and passing through all the illusions of fear, desire, anger and blame that Mara, the god of illusion, could set up before him, he reached his goal of Nirvana. He had moved through the illusory nature of the world to become the Buddha, the Enlightened One.

His journey then continued as he shared his understandings with those who would listen.

Clearing: An Introduction

Although I will reference this process often in the book, here is a brief introduction for those of you not familiar with this approach to working with energies, either personal or environmental.

Clearing arose initially from working with environmental energies, not the usual ones we associate with the environment but a much broader approach. This ranges from, but is not limited to, Earth energies, such as the Earth's magnetic field, to naturally occurring underground water and geological disturbances, to extremely low frequency electromagnetic fields including microwave radiation and how strong emotions, as charge, can be left in an environment, the metaphysical. All these have an effect, to some degree or other, on the residents of the space.

From working with environmental energies, a logical step was to begin to work with individuals. It became obvious to me, over the years that I have been practicing this approach, that as the environment affects us, in often unrealised or invisible ways, so we affect the environment. Each can be a mirror of the other. The challenge comes when the mirror is a little cloudy, caused by what Carl Jung refers to as the Shadow, more of that later in the book.

Essentially Clearing is about noticing how the body reacts/responds to any change in energy. Be that in a space or in the company of an individual. When we can rest, noticing how the body feels at any given time, generally limited to our capacity to notice, we can develop the ability to be more aware of how the body changes with various people or environments.

The practice asks us to be still and quiet, to notice what is happening in the body. We start with feelings, either physical or emotional. Once we have a baseline, it will allow us to notice any change that may arise in the body. Most of us are too busy, too preoccupied, living in the past or the future, to notice very much at all. That which we do notice is often the more powerful—i.e. intense feelings/emotions. When we experience these strong feelings or emotions, the chances are high that we identify with them. I am feeling this. I am feeling that. Etc.

This is the pattern most of us fall into. We identify with the feeling. Identifying with any feeling gives energy to that feeling and further intensifies it. Our conditioned mind is so used to taking all feelings personally that there is never a chance to reflect on the fact that these feelings may not actually belong to us.

When we are in a state of rest and either environmental conditions change or another person enters the room, we are able to notice the change as it is experienced in our body. This change is, simply put, the result of a different chemical entering the cells of the body.

These 'chemicals', I suspect, originate in the brain and are the result of particular neurons firing. The neuropeptides, as they are called (forgive my lack of knowledge about biology), are processed through the hypothalamus and turned into amino acids, which, I am informed, are the building blocks of life (Dr. Bruce Lipton). These amino acids, aka 'chemicals', then cascade through the body entering various cells.

This is then interpreted as a feeling or emotion. Clearing helps us see that the change in the body, as a result of circumstances outside of the body, is not something that 'belongs to us'; it is simply something that we are noticing.

If we were to continue to identify with the feeling, then basically that is giving energy to that feeling, which then makes it appear as though it is ours. If we can say to ourselves, 'This is the feeling of . . . ,' we do not create more chemicals that would otherwise create the impression, due to intensity of the feeling, that this is 'ours'.

Over time, with a lot of practice, the body gets used to just noticing change but no longer identifies with the many feelings that pass through its awareness in the course of the day. This then allows the body to experience a lot of feelings that would otherwise be judged and identified with. The broader range of feelings we can experience without giving them anymore energy, the safer we become with those feelings. Meaning as we no longer take them personally, they no longer control our lives, albeit on a subconscious level.

In turn this allows a lot of the hidden feelings, Jung's Shadow, to lose their intensity, freeing us up from a conditioned past that we were not even aware we had.

This is important if we are to move out of a conditioned past into a new future. I do not believe it is possible to move into a new future while we still see life through eyes influenced by the Shadow, the unloved, unknown aspects of self.

More of all this, in more detail, later in the book.

The Shadow

Something else that may help with a deeper understanding as we move through this book is Carl Jung's work on the 'Shadow'.

I refer to this frequently throughout the book, so it may help to get an insight before you dive into the rest of the book.

My current understanding of this is that any aspect of the self that we have not yet integrated into our conscious awareness remains hidden in the subconscious. There are many reasons why we have not yet brought these parts of the self into the light of conscious awareness. Primarily because they are in the subconscious, obviously this means that we are not aware of them.

During childhood, and possibly beyond, our ability to deal with some of the events life presents falls short; we are just not able, because we lack either awareness, emotional maturity or the physical strength to handle some situations. It seems to me that no part of our journey is lost. If we are unable to handle situations for any of the above reasons, then that information gets stored in the subconscious.

For example: Should you have suffered abuse at the hands of a sibling while you were still very young, you would not have the ability to recognise what was happening, nor the power to 'do' anything about it. This equates to a very powerful, deep impression being made upon the young child, an impression that they will carry for the rest of their lives.

This experience is going to influence that person on a very fundamental level, in many ways that the child/young adult will not even recognise because they have grown up in such a hostile environment that it has become a part of them; no longer does that person have the ability to be objective about those early years.

Trauma comes in many forms and varying degrees of intensity. It could be psychological, emotional or physical, or any combination of these. It could be an idea reinforced over and over again. Not good enough, not pretty enough, not smart enough.

It might simply be being born into a marginalised society with a history of persecution. You might be conditioned to see the world as a violent place, as an anxious society. From the point of view of the Shadow, it matters not what programming you underwent as a child.

While information remains buried in the subconscious, it will continue to play a major part in shaping that person's life. This is the Shadow.

Any experience that we were unable to process effectively will end up in the Shadow and contribute to the experiences that person undergoes.

Jung once commented that we do not become enlightened by imagining figures of light but by making the darkness conscious. He went on to say that this process is disagreeable and therefore not very popular.

I can understand it not being very popular, as any memories of trauma are not something anyone wants to revisit. There are ways though to bring this information into the light of conscious awareness that are not disagreeable. Those methods are non-confrontational. Indeed how can we confront that which we do not know we have. Impossible, right?

One of the paths we need to tread if we are to get even close to this Death-Less State is to learn how to embrace the Shadow so that we may be free of old conditioning, no longer a victim to our past. This is covered later in the book, but it may take more than reading a book to reach this understanding.

More is offered for those who would seek the Death-Less State. Your path, your choice.

Both Clearing and the Shadow play big parts in this journey as we seek the Death-Less State; they will be mentioned often throughout the book and are fundamental to our understanding.

In a few words from the 'Dzogchen Practice', by HH Dilgo Khyentse Rinpoche:

> 'The everyday practice is simply to develop
> a complete acceptance and openness to all situations
> and emotions and to all people, experiencing
> everything totally without mental reservations
> and blockages, so that one never withdraws
> or centralises into oneself.'

Even though the words in this book lead us into areas of discovery into the very nature of this human experience, and beyond, ultimately 'we will always find what we are looking for' (Richard Alpert, aka Ram Dass). This eventually becomes a problem, for while we seek something, while we try to understand something, we will always find that which we are searching for.

To know the Death-Less State then, we should stop searching, stop looking for anything in particular and remain open, unquestioning, resting in the stillness of a quiet mind. This is the challenge, to exhaust the inquiring mind, be still and observe.

Now see if these words help you reach that state.

And on with the journey.

Our Journey

We all have a journey, whether it takes us deeper into the world of illusion or leads us out of the illusory world. This is the story of my journey, as I too seek the Death-Less State, a state where we do not fall asleep when the body dies. A state where consciousness remains an unbroken thread or pure awareness, no longer subject to the vagaries of Greed, Fear, Ignorance or Desire, but instead can rest in the True Nature of Mind.

This journey is not for everyone, at least not at this time; it may well come to pass that all sentient beings recognise the value in such a path, but currently it seems as though identification with the thoughts and emotions associated with the self offers the most important paths to follow. Desire to understand the benefits to be gained by following a path that leads to an end to suffering is far from most minds, so lost are they in playing their part, reading the script that they believe to be who they are, that to recognise a different way of being in this world is not a concept they can even begin to understand.

When your time comes to begin this journey, when that little alarm bell is heard, when a realisation that there can be an end to suffering arises in your awareness, then other doors, previously hidden, begin to open, new possibilities in life arise, different people show up on your path, and slowly, oh so slowly, a new reality presents itself.

I say slowly because having spent many years on this path of self-discovery and through my own practice of Clearing or acceptance of whatever arises on my path (this concept is clarified later), I have come to see that the only blocks to our understanding this way of being is our addictions to old habits, which have led to a powerful sense of the self that identifies with all phenomena through the eyes of personality. We become creatures of habit; we learn to expect the world to be a certain way, be it a peaceful one or one full of conflict. We are taught how to survive in this world; we are taught separation, me, mine—you, yours. I am feeling this; I am thinking that. These are my feelings; these are my thoughts.

This conditioning, which we all seem to have to go through, sets the stage for our journey through life. The more polarised or radical our upbringing, the more we judge the behaviour of others as we compare it to our own values, perceptions, beliefs about how the world is or how it should be in order for our beliefs to be validated.

Yet those with a different background, a different way of seeing life, will be just as determined to create a world in which they feel safe, validated. This group comes into conflict with other groups who think differently, and conflict is inevitable. If history is to be believed, our life on planet Earth has been filled with one conflict or another for as long as there are writings to record our history. If we step back a moment to see the nature of conflict, it is always the same, one group opposing another group as they try to impose their values on the other, which is often resisted leading to open conflict. Nothing seems to have changed in hundreds, thousands, of years.

Not all peoples are in such strong conflict; there is a lot of beauty in this world, both natural and created by the human mind/hand. Yet even those who are not involved in conflict suffer, indirectly, the effects of those who are in conflict. Is there a way out of this suffering?

The Buddha thought so. A lot of his teachings were about the nature of suffering, the cause of suffering and the path that led to an end of suffering.

I read a lot of books on this when I was young. When I look back on those times, I am embarrassed by just how little I truly understood the teachings. But that was a part of my journey; coming out of the ignorance that was my life took many years—and is not over yet! Now I can see that the time it has taken me to reach my current understandings was because of my strong association with the sense of self, my conditioned past. Were it not for the habits developed in early years, and the continued identification with those habits, I could have 'woken up' a long time ago.

The more time I spend dedicated to this path, the more I understand how more amazing this journey is. So much becomes clearer; my world opens, as do my eyes. The part I play in creating the world we live in becomes more obvious, and with that understanding comes more responsibility. And as I reduce personal judgements so less conflict shows up on my path, I meet more open, smiling faces, challenging situations cease to arise and the path unfolds effortlessly.

My journey is by no means unique; the path I have taken may be.

The Mind

Thus have I heard/read/experienced.

Any journey, no matter where to or why, must involve The Mind. How we think plays a major part in creating the world we live in. So understanding The Mind can help us understand how we create, what and why we create.

Many years ago I read a book by Dr. Larry Dossey, *Recovering the Soul*. In it he spoke of The Mind being non-local. This was a fascinating insight, imagined intellectually, but the real impact of such a statement has only become 'real' with time and walking this path.

Assuming The Mind is non-local, what does this actually mean? Well to me 'non-local' means not confined in time or space, meaning The Mind is everywhere, at all times. Picture this as a great Sea of Consciousness. Many people have given it a name in the past, The Mind of God, The Field—different religions have different names, all meaning the same thing. Personally I prefer referring to it as the Cosmic Soup.

Now if we bother to explore this concept and tie it in with various teachings through the ages and listen to some of the more influential minds of recent times, we hear such comments as:

> 'The objective world arises from the mind itself.'
> The Buddha

> 'Every man's world picture is and always remains a construct of his mind and cannot be proved to have any other existence.'
> Erwin Schrödinger

The list goes on. Taking this idea on board as a possible truth, we then go looking for the personal mind—'my' mind. But I am not convinced we are going to be able to find this elusive personal mind. If indeed The Mind is non-local, then how can it be contained within this body? If you think you have a mind, where is it? Point it out! A clue, it is not the brain.

I currently believe that we, individually, do not have a mind. This runs contrary to popular thinking of course. We are so used to associating thoughts with our mind—we use 'our' mind; we put 'our' mind to solving a problem; we make up 'our' mind. Yet consider the possibility for a moment that you do not have a mind. What you do have is a nervous system, brain included, that has the ability to access this non-local Mind. You might want to think about that for a moment or two!

If this indeed is what is happening, then it opens all sorts of questions and possibilities.

The Buddha was reported to have said:

'Since everything is a product of one's own mind...'

Now who really knows if he said this or someone else did, but it does connect some dots as we try to understand the nature of The Mind. If this was a comment by the Buddha, then I cannot fully support it. I think the word 'mind' here is used to describe a thinking, discriminating person's abilities. Many people's only point of reference is their own mind and cannot be any other way. Yet if we consider that Mind is indeed non-local, then what part of this Mind are we? Is this mind split into millions of pieces with each of us having a part of The Mind? I have trouble accepting this basing my understanding of a non-local Mind.

Allow me to try and explain my point of view.

Imagine for a moment that, as mentioned above, we do not have a personal/individual mind; instead we have a body with a unique nervous system and brain.

The Nervous System Accessing The Mind

It is our nervous system that accesses the non-local mind. We see shape (those of us fortunate enough to 'see'), form and colour; we hear sounds (again those fortunate enough to be able to hear).

We taste; we pick up different fragrances; we touch and we 'feel'.

We analyse (think about), through our brain, the information that we detect through the nervous system. Then, based upon childhood conditioning, we judge that which we detect.

As we judge, associate or identify with the information the body senses, the neurons in the brain fire in an often already established order; we call this habit learnt behaviour. A conditioned reaction to information creates a unique neuropeptide. (This is based upon my understanding of the work of Dr. Bruce Lipton—I could never be a cellular biologist!) In turn these neuropeptides are turned into amino acids, apparently the building blocks of life, again according to my understanding of Dr. Lipton's work.

The amino acids then cascade through the body and, depending upon the developed nature of the cells, enter the cell, changing the cell to some degree or other. The result is what we call a feeling—either physical or emotional. Then through our past conditioning—me, mine, you, yours, etc.—we identify with the feeling. I am feeling this; I am feeling that. This identification process, in Buddhism, is called desire and grasping. Meaning when a feeling arises in the body, we immediately identify with it, claiming it to be ours. Whether we like it or not, want it or not.

This, according to Dr. Lipton, and I am sure others, has the effect of intensifying the feeling. What this means, in my very limited understanding of this subject, is that when the individual cell divides into sister cells, the new cell has more receptor sites on it for the certain chemicals that we associate with the feeling we identified with. The receptor site is like a small antenna that is tuned to a very specific frequency. The door can only be opened with the right key.

Many of us may tend to view these chemicals as physical matter, albeit tiny particles of matter. We give them names to help understand them, but as I strongly suspect, these chemicals are actually matter operating at highly specific frequencies. A chemical, an amino acid in this case, resonates with the receptor site on the cell, and then, through a protein link which connects the receptor to an acceptor, the cell allows the chemical to enter the cell. We interpret this as a feeling. Identifying with a feeling, i.e. an emotion, instructs the cell; then when it subdivides, it allows more receptor sites for that particular chemical, which in turn intensifies the feeling. The more of any particular chemical that enters the cells, the more intense the feeling appears to be. The more intense the feeling, the more we identify with it as being 'ours'.

This information becomes more important as we begin to understand the nature of our experience, and we will see how it ties into our journey towards the Death-Less State later in the book.

So by identifying with any particular emotion, we increase the body's ability to experience a more intense emotion. I have seen so many people talk themselves into an emotional state. Talking about a state or condition is, on some level, identifying with that state, which then basically instructs the brain to produce more of these chemicals. The result is that those amino acids/chemicals enter the cells, which we then identify with. The more we talk about a situation or emotion—the more time and energy we give to any particular feeling—the more intense it becomes.

Simply put, we are telling the brain to produce more of the chemicals we are identifying with. Following this reasoning, we can see how we are creating an internal reality based upon how strongly we associate with particular feelings, both good and not so good.

There is another side to this process, a more insidious side. In my, again limited, understanding of this process, I understand that there is very limited space on the cell for these receptor sites. The cell is pretty small, so the receptor sites have to be unimaginably small, and room on the cell for the receptor sites is limited. Following this reasoning, if we fill the cell wall with receptor sites of a specific frequency through our habit of identifying with certain emotions, then we must 'bump' other receptor sites, no more room at the inn!

If we take depression as an example, it becomes easier to understand how, by continued identification with a feeling or emotion (or thought!), that feeling grows. Knowingly or not—most likely not—our conditioning tells us to identify with everything we experience. This association with phenomena or feelings is controlled via the subconscious, Carl Jung's 'Shadow'. Because of our conditioned past, we may identify with the chemical of depression, meaning neurons fire as a result of a certain stimuli thus creating a neuropeptide which creates an amino acid, it is this chemical that enters the cell giving rise to a 'feeling' or an emotion. If we associate the amino acid, the chemical, with depression and we take that feeling personally then the sister cells of the original cell that took this chemical, aka information, in will have more receptor sites for depression as they continue to subdivide. All this leads to a more depressed state.

As some of you may know, depression is a pretty low energy feeling; it appears to drain vitality out of the body, reducing our will to 'do' anything. Bad enough, you might think, but try to imagine what is happening to the cells in the body. You are, by the conscious or subconscious identification with the feeling of depression, reducing the cell's ability to operate in a healthy manner. No room on the cell for many of the receptor sites the body needs to function in a healthy manner. This in turn only adds to the feeling of depression, making it harder to get out of.

It is also opening up the body to a state of ill health because the body is no longer able to fend off more of the low-energy feelings/chemicals that may well be associated with other health problems. This may compromise the immune system, the body's natural ability to fight disease, which will lead to other complications.

The deeper into any emotional state (still referring to emotions for the time being) we go, the more potential damage we are doing to the body. The deeper we go down any particular rabbit hole, the harder it becomes to get ourselves out of the hole. Not only are we dealing with the symptoms associated with any particular chemical; we are also faced with the thinking that allowed this situation to develop. All this time we fail to realise that we are lost down the rabbit hole, our current thinking does not allow for this world view.

As Einstein once said:

> 'We cannot solve the problem
> from the thinking that created it.'

But surely no one would have given energy to, for example, depression if they had any say in it.

As I understand it, there are two unconscious conditions in play here. They both affect our ability to remain in a healthy state, physically, emotionally and mentally. One, the obvious one, is our conditioning.

When we were very young, we went through the process of being born and then educated into what it meant, according to our parents and society in general, to be a person. This will be a whole other chapter later where we look in more detail about what this actually means in a more global sense. For the time being though, individuals are taught that feelings are theirs, thoughts are theirs, some possessions are theirs, and so it goes.

The other major driving force causing us to appear to be victims to feelings beyond our ability to control would be what Jung has referred to as 'our Shadow'.

Basically the Shadow is made up of aspects of the self that we have not yet acknowledged and brought into conscious awareness. These are subconscious aspects of the self, meaning that we are not aware of them. With no awareness of these parts of the self, we can do nothing about them. Failing to even recognise that they exist, we remain victims to them.

Jung said, I believe, that while we remain unaware of these aspects of self, we will continue to experience the symptoms, or results, of these aspects and believe the experiences that arise out of this condition to be our fate. In actual fact they are simply parts of ourselves coming back to us, parts that we fail to recognise or accept. This whole process leads to us blaming others for any discomfort that we experience.

Having been conditioned that anything we feel is 'ours', then it is hardly surprising that when any particular emotion arises in our awareness, we associate, identify, with it. As we have already noted, if we continue to give that feeling energy, we will create a more intense feeling, some of which feels good to us, others not so good.

Later we can look at how this continued identification with any feeling creates both the internal and external reality that we are able to perceive.

It appears then that we are not really in the driver's seat of our life. We may be in the back seat trying to tell the driver where to go, when to turn, when to stop, but our efforts to override the main driving force only complicates our lives. All the time that we fail to recognise that many of our thoughts, words, actions are outside of our conscious control, we will continue to fight against our 'fate', failing to recognise that we continually sabotage and create complications.

It seems to me as though there are some serious flaws in our early conditioning and education, forcing us to be victims to circumstances that appear to be beyond our control. Who was it though who created who we believe ourselves to be now? We could say our parents and society in general, but they were just following the program they were indoctrinated into. How far back do we need to go to get answers?

Although if this human experience is mostly to go deep into separation and individuality in order for The Mind to experience The Mind, then there are no flaws, no mistakes; it is all unfolding as it should. We go in, we come out, eventually. It is the coming out of the identification with the experience that seems to be difficult, and many will question why we need to come out of the experience. I personally don't think we have that choice. I think conditions that keep us lost in the drama that is our life are self-perpetuating—remember the Shadow and the subconscious where we are victims to circumstance? I suspect that circumstances are always conspiring to wake us up, and yet our addictions and habits are so strong that we fail to recognise the signs that are constantly 'knocking on the door'. For if the Mind is non-local, meaning everywhere at all times, no beginning, no end, then that which we believe we are looking for is here now, not waiting down the road for us, not waiting for a few years, or lifetimes, but right here, right now.

What Do You Believe?

*More and more I see how our thoughts
create the world we live in.*

Our thoughts are shaped, fundamentally, by our early childhood; we are conditioned by parents and society to believe certain ways of being. Our parents, in their turn, were conditioned by their parents and their society. Oftentimes parents simply pass on the beliefs that were passed on to them. No one questions fundamental beliefs outside of the framework within which they believe they exist.

Where and when you were born, what type of society you grew up in, what religious background you have if any, what social conditions rich or poor, your language, the colour of your skin: These are all conditions that go into the melting pot of your personality. More conditions to consider: Your view of the world, your relationships with others on either a personal or social level, the strength of your beliefs. Did you grow up in a supportive environment, or were you undermined by parents and society because you were 'different'?

Remember your parents and society in general have also been through a similar process. Their world view, as is yours, was shaped by the circumstances in which they grew up. We are all—until we are not—victims to our past. We cannot blame those who came into this world before us for they too have much in their Shadow; they too are lost in the drama that is their life.

I believe it is the intensity of our conditioning that creates situations that appear to be real in this world. Situations so apparently real that we are forced to do something about them in order to create a world that supports our very polarised view of how the world should be, needs to be, in order for us to feel safe and valued.

This gets pretty complicated when, in addition to the points of view of the society into which we are born, our personal points of view are heavily coloured by any traumatic experiences—real or imagined—that we went though in those early childhood years.

Combine these and we get a unique individual, either compensating for these real or supposed traumas in early life or becoming even more polarised members of society.

The more polarised we become, for whatever reason, the more judgemental we get. The more judgemental, the more we blame the 'other', whoever the 'other' may be, for any discomfort we may feel. This means, on a personal level, we are feeding certain chemical processes, creating more intense feelings. The more intense the feeling, the more we have to act to balance out that feeling. If we believe that by hurting the other it will make us feel better about ourself or become a more valued member of our society, then we take stronger action to create the world that we personally believe to be the 'right' one.

Of course on the other side of this fence, be it a personal or intimate relationship, a group of people holding different points of view, a neighbouring village, country, religion, political party, whatever, then the people with these differing points of view may well believe they are right and their point of view should be the dominating factor to make their world a 'better' place—and then conflict is inevitable.

It all comes down to a point of view, mine being better than yours!

When we understand where a point of view comes from and why it is perpetuated, we may begin to see that on one level all points of view are valid, no one point of view being any better than any other. Yet all the time we remain locked into the self-created prison of personality, we will see ourselves as separate individuals, all trying hard to make everyone else conform to our point of view and therefore perpetuating conflict and thus creating more opposition from groups who hold different points of view.

But What Is a Point of View?

This world, according to our perceptions, appears to be speeding up. Technology has changed our lives in a very short time, certainly in my lifetime so many changes, all happening so fast. It can be a challenge keeping up; the pace of life seems to be a lot faster now than it was when I was a child. Instant communication and sharing of ideas and points of view are both readily available due to advances in technology. Whether this speeding up is real or imagined, the results are the same.

The situations and experiences in our lives seem to have less time to sort themselves out; we are under more pressure to conform to a fast-changing society. The human body is put under a lot of pressure. Maybe it was in the past, but we were not so aware then. Technology has made us more aware.

Any system, be it mechanical, electrical or the human body, has certain stress safety levels built in—certain tolerances within which it can safely operate. When these tolerances are exceeded, the system starts to fail, to malfunction; and if the cause of the additional stress is not addressed, then the system will eventually collapse.

Take a garden hose with water running through it. Bend the hose and hold it tightly, stopping the flow of water. Water still wants to flow but cannot because you have crimped the hose causing pressure to build. When the pressure gets to a certain point, any weakness in the system will be exposed and will break, allowing the water to flow again, just not out the end of the hose where it was supposed to. Any mechanical or electrical system will do the same.

The human body is no different. If stress is allowed to build because there is no awareness that stress is building until it becomes obvious, then any weakness in the system is exploited. This may be because we have not developed a sufficiently reliable stress relief valve or we unconsciously add stress to the body (by overly identifying with certain 'negative' emotions). The body will then show signs of the stress, and eventually it will be obvious that the body is failing to deal with stress and sickness or disease will present.

Symptoms of a stressed body can be physical, emotional or mental. Burnout being an obvious and quite common symptom, with other symptoms being high levels of anxiety, panic attacks, emotional rage or major physical heath issues, to name just a few of the symptoms of a stressed body.

If the person who is experiencing any symptoms of stress is still in judgement of others—blaming others for their own condition—then the more stressed their system becomes, the more likely it is that they will create more conflict, further aggravating their own condition by increasing the number of receptor sites on the cell, thereby reducing the number and type of receptor sites the body needs to remain healthy. This does seem to be the way of the world for many.

A Computer Simulation?

It has been proposed, by some, that we live in a computer simulation. An interesting theory that has only recently arisen, mainly because computers are a relatively recent addition to our vocabulary. What language might have been used to describe the world we live in before the invention of computers?

Or as may be possible, computers have always existed in The Mind, just waiting to be discovered—remember the non-local mind.

Many ways of describing phenomena in this world change with the language of the times. I read, several years ago, a book called the *Holographic Universe* by Michael Talbot discussing the life and works of David Bohm, theoretical physicist, and Karl Pribram, neurosurgeon and professor of psychology. In it Talbot looked at both of their individual approaches to try to better understand The Mind and how our reality is created.

Coming from different directions, both men, according to Talbot, came to similar conclusions. That conclusion was that we live in a hologram. Or because this world is continually unfolding, not a static image produced by a hologram, it has been named a Holoverse.

Very simply put, and I rely on a not too accurate memory now, this Holoverse describes a multiverse created out of the input, keeping it simple, of human consciousness.

A hologram is a three-dimensional image taken using a laser, a coherent beam of light. The image is captured on a two-dimensional photographic plate. This image, unlike a regular photographic image that is made up of many coloured pixels, consists of a complex series of whorls and concentric circles. This image means nothing until a beam of light, the laser of an identical coherence, is shined through it; the result is a three-dimensional projection of the image in space.

If you broke a regular photographic plate into a million pieces, you would end up with a part of a pixel that in no way would reflect the original image. If you did the same to a holographic plate, then each part of the broken plate would contain the same information as that of the complete plate, a little fuzzy maybe, but it would be an otherwise accurate representation of the original image.

This becomes important when we see the part each of us plays in the creation of the unfolding hologram. We are all parts of the whole, contributing to the whole; and fascinatingly so, we all contain the information of the whole. Ultimately what this may mean is that we are truly Omniscient; All Knowing; Omnipresent; Ever Present and Omnipotent; All Powerful. Which, in my understanding, is the Death Less State, or the true understanding of the nature of the mind referred to in Buddhism. So this state, or the access to this state, already exists within us. We are that state, right now, whether we realise it or not.

We could call this non-local mind the Holoverse. Information is fed in, reacted to and then fed back.

It is the wave pattern we see on a holographic plate that creates the world we 'appear' to live in. The concentric circles and other patterns formed on the holographic plate create what is called an interfering wave pattern. An interference will present when a laser of the same resonant frequency that created it (in our example that would be an individual's perception) is passed through that plate. It is the resulting interfering wave pattern that creates the world the individual lives in. Whereas a hologram is a static image, the Holoverse is a continual unfolding.

Imagine standing around a great pond; we can call this for simplicity's sake the Ocean of the (non-local) Mind, or as I prefer the Sea of Consciousness. Many names have been given to this pond. You throw a pebble into the pond, and the waves that are formed, as the pebble hits the surface of the pond, ripple out in an ever expanding pattern. If you were the only being throwing pebbles into the pond, those ripples would continue to expand until they reached the other side of this hypothetical pond when they would react with the distant shoreline and bounce back. As the waves we sent out meet other waves, they would form the interfering wave pattern, bringing into being a response or a reaction to the original pebble.

Imagine that original pebble was an emotion—an energetic expression of something you felt strongly about. An emotion is a transference of energy; it is not something that is contained within the body that originates the emotion. Like a radio station sending out radio waves, we, humanity, are sending out our own signals, either emotional, mental or physical. So all our thoughts, feelings, words and actions are transmissions into this Sea of Consciousness, and they all return to us.

This idea, when taken further, implies that whatever we put into the Sea comes back to us. This serves to reinforce our belief that whatever is put in is real and supports the idea that our thoughts and emotions are indeed real and that we are right in believing in them. When, in reality, the Sea is simply feeding back to us whatever is put in, having nothing to do with right or wrong, good or bad. It is simply a powerful biological feedback device.

So we get back what we put in. This idea gives rise to the current beliefs that we create our own reality and can therefore create health, wealth and happiness, or anything in between! Lots of programs out there today instruct you how to do that.

Oh if It Were So Simple

Things begin to get complicated when you realise that you are not the only person throwing pebbles into the pond. Every sentient being on this planet is either consciously or unconsciously, or both, throwing pebbles into the pond. As you might imagine, this creates a great confusion of interfering wave patterns that is fed back into an individual's consciousness, confusing the issue of who created the reality.

Now imagine millions of people all throwing similar pebbles into the pond. This has the effect of feeding back the idea that whatever this collective is putting in is indeed reality. So far so good. But what happens when millions of people with two opposing points of view all throw their own unique pebbles into the pond? Major interfering wave patterns arise.

Because of the nature of the pond's response or reaction, this interfering wave pattern is very intense. This forces the original group of millions to throw bigger pebbles into the pond in an attempt to influence, or exert their perceptions over, the very nature of the manifesting reality. Of course the other millions defend their beliefs by responding with bigger pebbles of their own.

There are many players in this game, many belonging to specific groups, all throwing pebbles into the pond expressing their own ideals of what a perfect world should look like.

Imagine you have an idea. Perhaps it is that eating tulips on the third Friday of the month is really good for you. Strange, but I have heard stranger beliefs! Now you convince a few friends that this is a good thing. You and your friends put this idea into the pond, but it has little impact upon the many wave forms already existing in the pond. Remember you get back what you throw in, and this Mind is an amazing place; it does not judge your input.

Another group believes instead that eating roses on the second Tuesday of the month is the way to go. Because there are so few believers in these ideas, the feedback is minimal and the idea does not gain any real traction. These ideas have no real impact upon the bigger picture.

If your group of believers grows, then so does the number of pebbles that are thrown into the pond relating to your idea. This may meet with the conflicting stories of the believers in the rose, causing some conflict which can, given enough energy, spill over into the world and result in open conflict. This is happening to all beliefs/pebbles that are thrown into the pond.

If this process continues to escalate, we will then have groups throwing bigger stones into the pond — bombs and missiles. What sort of reaction from this powerful biofeedback device, that is The Mind, will this create? More of the same of course, as all the time those who are throwing sticks and stones into the pond fail to recognise the nature of their actions—that they are simply adding to the resulting chaos/confusion/conflict. All the time that individuals remain selfishly unaware of their actions on the bigger picture, the energy given to conflict continues to grow. Or are they really unaware? Or is this a deliberate action to create the illusion of more wealth and power?

It certainly appears that the pond is not judging individuals for their actions.

Possibly the challenge that we all face is to stop reacting to the results of the interfering wave patterns. All the time we react, whether consciously or unconsciously, we perpetuate the drama that is unfolding. By our reactions to this manifesting reality, we continue to throw pebbles into the pond, supporting one side, one team, one belief over another. This must, in this model, add more energy to the wave forms, creating even more powerful reactions.

This seems to have been the pattern throughout the history of this planet, that we know of anyway. One group wants control for example; another group opposes the control. More pebbles are thrown into the pond until one group or both eradicate the other. The drama doesn't end there of course. Individuals who suffer the result of any conflict remember—they hold grudges which colour the stones that they in their turn throw into the pond.

And on it goes.

Back to the individual who is trying to sort out a way through all these interfering wave patterns. A challenge indeed to not take sides, our own sense of righteousness overrules our common sense, not deliberately, not on purpose. For we all have been conditioned during our early years to hold certain values, believe certain ways of being are good, or bad. We have our personal likes and dislikes, all of which have been pebbles we threw, likely without awareness, into the Sea.

These early pebbles, thrown into the Sea without conscious awareness, all come back to us, supporting our points of view, giving a sense of rightness to that which we believe ourselves to be, further reinforcing the concept that we were right to believe certain things.

This feedback establishes and confirms our personality, which in turn naturally takes sides in any argument, because our reality is based upon that which we were instructed, albeit unconsciously, to believe and therefore affected the type of pebble, emotion, thought, word, action that we put into the Sea.

Quite the challenge, trying to sort out if there is any truth in any of the feedback we get. A challenge because the individual trying to sort out fact from fiction is already lost in the dream and is basing their responses on the idea of the truth on their conditioned past, which has been reinforced by the feedback it gets back from the energy it has put into the Sea.

Truly a Dilemma

A big part of the challenge we individuals face as we attempt to feed into the Sea that which will return greater health, wealth or happiness is that we are sabotaging our own efforts. This is not a conscious sabotage—that would be crazy; rather it is because any motivation we have to change our circumstances is based on discontent with what we have already. We always want more, of whatever.

We fail to get more because of aspects of the self—back to Jung's Shadow—that we have yet to embrace, accept, bring into the light of consciousness. All these parts of the self are also contributing to our reality by throwing pebbles into the pond. This may explain why we do not always get what we want. In fact a lot of the feedback we do get is opposed to what we want, situations of conflict and/or challenges to our way of being. This gives rise to situations or people that show up in our lives to create discontent or open conflict.

As a result of early childhood conditioning, certain experiences that the young child was not able, due to age, immaturity, etc,, to accept are hidden away, possibly because they are too painful, too upsetting, to acknowledge. This may well be the beginning of the formation of the

Shadow, although I believe that it is another step along the way of the individualisation of the person.

While we fail to acknowledge the part the Shadow plays in creating our personal reality, as mentioned earlier, we experience that which Jung called 'our fate'. We react against this by throwing yet another pebble into the pond. This is an attempt to neutralise the effects or the feedback that we get on a daily basis as a result of the earlier pebbles thrown into the Sea, both consciously and unconsciously.

Seems like a never-ending process, constantly trying to balance out the feedback by adding more pebbles.

The Buddha was reported to have said:

> 'Do not do or say anything that will create remorse.'

He said this because, I suspect, of the ongoing feedback associated with putting pebbles into the pond. Feedback which may create an energy of remorse and consequently bounce back to, in part, affect or even create your manifesting reality.

I can see the value of not reacting, based on the model of the Holoverse. I can also see the problems associated with not doing or saying anything that will create remorse. If we are not aware, not conscious, of the pebbles that the subconscious, the Shadow, throws into the pond, how can we be truly responsible for our thoughts, words or actions, or even our reactions to life's experiences? We think, do or say things from a conditioned past which includes the Shadow aspects of the self, of which by their very nature we are not aware. So it seems inevitable that we will create these same situations where remorse is not only possible, but inevitable.

All the time we remain unaware of these aspects of the self, we will continue to do or say things that are going to create remorse, suffer the consequences and react by throwing more pebbles of blame and judgement—of others or the self—into the pond, further complicating our lives as the feedback eventually arrives, once again reinforcing our belief in our own points of view.

It seems to me important that we begin to see the part we play, both consciously and unconsciously, in the creation of our personal reality. To begin, we must acknowledge that we have Shadow aspects of the self. Aspects that we do not know we have, their being hidden in our subconscious but present in our lives on a daily basis as problems, challenges, uncomfortable situations.

If we can see that who we believe ourselves to be is indeed a product of our own making, that which we have fed into the Sea, consciously or otherwise, has returned to show us exactly what we have been putting into the sea. This affirms our personal beliefs but not always in a way we like or approve of. Until we change the pebbles that we throw into the pond, our manifesting reality cannot change. All the time that we remain unaware of the part the Shadow plays in creating the world we live in, we will continue to create the same old problems.

If this is indeed how our realities are created, then I think it is incredibly important that as many people as possible realise this and see that many of our troubles are of our own making. There will always (?) be those who remain victims to the actions of others, seemingly innocent, I shall explore this innocence later.

Assuming that this Holoverse model is an accurate representation of how 'reality' is formed, then we do not live in a computer-generated reality but in a complex biofeedback device.

If we can agree, if only for a moment, that Mind is non-local, meaning it is everywhere at all times, containing all knowledge from the past and present, possibly the future as well, then the states of Omniscience, Omnipotence and Omnipresence are also possibilities that exist in the here and now. Then it is easy to see how this non-local Mind is a storehouse of vast knowledge and information. We may be feeding back our own knowledge and experiences, judgements and values into this Mind, which just may be how The Mind knows itself.

For without an objective observer, The Mind does not appear to exist. If we cannot stand outside of this Mind, we can never truly know it. Some people may refer to this Mind as God; others have chosen a different word. Yet I think that a good case has been made for its existence, especially if you research the subject and see just who has commented on it.

Accessing a Bigger Picture

Some figures from our distant past, more recent past and your present age have accessed knowledge and wisdom far beyond that of the majority. Could it be that their focus has been very specific, tuning into, if you will, certain knowledge that is, and always has been, held in The Mind and bringing that knowledge and wisdom back to share with the rest of humanity?

Is this what a skilled musician does? An artist? A scientist? An engineer? Is this what 'I' am doing?

Have I—for whatever reason, a few of those reasons will appear throughout the book—tuned into a source of wisdom way beyond what I imagined possible? Is this what any of us do? Because if we personally do not have a mind but instead have the ability to tune into The Mind, then the thoughts that we have are not our own; they did not originate within our mind. If we do not have an individual mind, then the thoughts must have come from somewhere outside of the self, The Mind. Yet we hold onto the belief that they are our thoughts, mainly because we have never been taught otherwise, because no reasonable option has shown up in our lives.

No reasonable option has shown up because of our often narrow focus. Our narrow focus arises out of the conditioning we have experienced, conditioning that was information passed on to us by others, our parents! Parents who themselves received information from their parents. Rarely is there an opportunity to break away from this consensus view of reality to understand what and why and how. People do explore the what, why and how; yet most do it from the perception of the limited human ability, one who is still taking that which they see as reality without realising that their search is itself within the bounds of limitation.

Even so, I call this exploring The Mind, possibly The Mind getting to know itself.

Where Your Attention Goes

It has become obvious to me that where we focus our awareness, we create our reality. We do this on a simple, personal level by changing the physiology of the body with changing thoughts, or directed awareness. If our focus remains on the past, we continue to repeat old patterns; all the time we do that, we are caught in a loop, likely of our own making. A loop that is continually requiring us to respond or react either in the same old way, rinse repeat, or in a different way, but any different way, any possible choice we may have, is still a product of past choices.

The conflict that we see happening around the planet is a product of the past—nothing just arises out of nothing; everything has a past. It may be obvious, but where there has been little or no understanding of this, stress builds in any system. In the case of open conflict, the stress has reached a level where the insecurity, which I believe is fundamental to the human condition, has reached such a point, the stress is no longer containable and explodes into open conflict.

Maybe conflict would be unnecessary if we were all to realise that we live in a Holoverse that all that presents in our reality arises out of information, in the form of thoughts, emotions, words and actions, that has been fed into the Holoverse in the past. Keep feeding the same information in and expect a world where conflict exists to continue to unfold.

To keep feeding the same information into this model and expect to find a happy, peaceful outcome is really rather naive. For those lost in the belief that a peaceful outcome is possible when you can dominate your corner of the world fail to understand that there are many parties who are also lost in the drama, who believe their ways are the only ways. This thinking will not stop all the while there is a sense of better than, righter than, more deserving than.

For all the players, lost in the drama, who take their roles so seriously and who die still strongly attached to the role they played, there is a price to pay.

For the game does not stop at death, which is why this information has been included in a book exploring the Death-Less State.

The Bardos

To my knowledge this is a Buddhist term meaning a Realm of Becoming.

What is a Realm of Becoming? For those with less understanding than myself, I offer this: For the moment accept that The Mind is non-local, a vast storehouse of information, past, present and future, and that the Holoverse is a reasonably accurate description of how our reality is created. Having accepted this, then we see how our continued input into The Mind, the Holoverse, creates the world we live in.

The next thing to accept would be that we are not the isolated individuals that we currently believe ourselves to be. Instead we are a part of The Mind, an active part of The Mind. We access information from The Mind. We feed back information to The Mind. Quite possibly we are all aspects of the divine.

Know that when you experience an emotion, the stronger the emotion, the more obvious the result. Depending upon your levels of sensitivity, you may have walked into a room where a strong argument is happening, or happened very recently. You can feel the change in the energy in the room; it may be an uncomfortable feeling for you. But there is definitely the feeling of emotional charge in the room.

What has happened, I believe, is one or both (maybe more) parties involved in the conflict have been strongly identifying with a particular feeling. Back to my basic biology, when we notice a feeling in the body, our conditioned response is to identify with that feeling—whether we are conscious of doing this or not! Obviously if we are not aware we are doing this, we remain a victim to our subconscious, the Shadow, or past conditioning.

Most of the time we cannot help ourselves; we cannot simply stand back and look at the chemical reactions going on in the body in an objective way. More often than not, these are feelings that we are familiar with, meaning we have experienced them before. The more often they have happened in the past, the more reactive we become. The more reactive we are, the less time there is to simply notice the body's chemistry changing and we are quickly lost in the emotion.

A noticeable change in body chemistry occurs when a chemical, amino acids in this case, enters the cells in the body; we experience this as, for example, anger.

Because we identify with the body and its emotions, we believe that we are angry. This simply lets the brain know—a brain that is not standing in judgement of that which you identify with—to produce more neuropeptides, which in turn create more amino acids that, when they enter the cells, create an even more intense feeling of anger.

This makes us feel more anger, so now we think we are very angry (you can exchange 'anger' for any emotion you wish). By identifying with the chemical of more anger, this creates more chemicals; the more chemicals created, the more angry we become. This process continues until it explodes in an outward expression of this anger.

Now imagine that the physiology of the body is changing, from a peaceful state to a very angry state. You notice when you encounter a peaceful person, and your body reacts to the peacefulness. It feels comfortable, no threat to you, and consequently your body reacts to that state. The same happens when you encounter an angry, or anxious, person. Your body responds, or reacts, to the energy of the other. Even though nothing has been said, there is a subconscious reaction to what I believe to be an energetic transmission.

Then it should be obvious that your body is reacting to information that is not observable, but instead to an energetic transmission.

Now picture that energetic transmission as a pebble being dropped into The Mind, or the Holoverse, or whatever name you prefer to call this field, this Quantum Soup. The ripples from this pebble spread out, affecting not only the people nearby but everyone in the pond to a lesser degree. These ripples interact with all the other ripples in the pond, creating the interfering wave pattern, which is fundamental to the creation of a hologram, or in our case a Holoverse. This reality, that we have unconsciously sent out into the pond, comes back to us, an unpleasant reality, forcing us to respond, often with a bigger pebble. And so it goes. All the time trying to balance out the effects of the pebbles we have previously tossed into the pond.

It seems, then, that if this is true, then we are a community dealing with symptoms that arise, all the time unaware of the real cause of those symptoms. All the while we treat symptoms and ignore the cause, there are always going to be more symptoms to treat. I do not believe the origin, the fundamental cause of the symptoms we face today, is to be found by looking into our past.

If everything is a product of The Mind and has no basis in reality, simply what we perceive to be reality, then it must be illusory in that it was created by previous pebbles thrown into the pond. Trying to understand or make sense of an illusion instead of seeing through it surely is like trying to understand or make sense of a children's fairy story.

If we continue to give energy to our past in order to understand it, we are simply keeping it alive. If instead we were to practice putting our attention on a different reality, meaning we change the pebbles we throw into the pond, we would create a different reality, one that does not support the past. A far better use of our time surely.

A Challenging Concept

There will likely be many objections to this approach, mostly by those trained or conditioned to believe that understanding the past is the way forward. Again, what you put into The Mind comes back to you, reinforcing your belief that your points of view are valid. It is the nature of the world we live in. I suspect that we live in a make-it-up-as-you-go type of universe. So anything you put in appears valid and confirms your original beliefs. Following this understanding, everything, every approach, every method, works. The only limitations are how many people believe that works. How many subscribers do you have who support your beliefs?

Easy to see advertising and propaganda as a means to get your vote; the more votes you have, the more 'real' your projections appear.

We are all exploring The Mind, a Mind which has no judgement, no boundaries. What you put in you get back. The more stones thrown into the pond by those believing in a certain healing modality, for example, the more powerful it becomes. If this leads to greater attachment to the association or identification with the body as being responsible in any way, then it is likely to not lead to the Death-Less State; rather it will take you on an ongoing exploration of consciousness through separation, i.e. into another body. The power of any modality is simply an expression of The Mind, which appears to be infinite. The range of study of this Mind is without end. The only limits are those imposed by the imagination of the individuals and the stones they throw into the pond, the access where they put their attention or focus on.

So when the Buddhists refer to the True Nature of Mind, what do they mean? Are we not already a part of that Mind; surely it cannot be any other way! We are already an aspect of The Mind. The only difference I can imagine would be that we are only accessing a very small part of The Mind, that which we consciously or otherwise focus on. This focus is very much associated with a personality, one which observes a small part of The Mind and taking seriously, personally, that which it observes. In other words, we take personally the feedback we get from The Mind, or Holoverse.

This is what we believe to be real, but it is only a very limited understanding of The Mind simply because the observer, the personality, is still seeing it through very conditioned eyes. And as brilliant as the human can be, we are still limited in what we can see and how we can understand.

According to Buddhist teachings, we literally lose our 'minds' when we are born. This implies that we were in the state of the True Nature of Mind before we were born. Personally I am not so sure we were aware of this, and that requires another paragraph!

Clearing and the Practice of Acceptance

Much of what I write about I have read in books that crossed my path; yet the real understanding that has developed has come from other places.

As a result of my work Clearing—which is essentially the practice of acceptance—many 'layers' of personality have fallen away. These aspects of personality are not real, just that which I came to believe to be real about who I was because of past conditioning.

Imagine a newborn, still in a state of one-ness developing the skills to survive in a body but also being given information and experiences that shape the path of that individual on their journey through life. Not all of the information is beneficial; much of it is just hearsay passed on from generation to generation. If the growing child experiences any trauma, real or imagined, that is going to have a major effect on that child's journey.

We can call these layers that go to make up the personality a filter system. We see the world through eyes conditioned by that which we are taught and that which we experience. These filter systems obviously colour the experience. For example, if you were born into a violent household, you would be conditioned to see the world as a violent place. I have worked with people who see the world through the filter system of violence; it is not a happy world. There are many filter systems through which different people experience their lives. The problem with filter systems is that they condition the individual to come to expect the world to be a certain way. With the expectation comes the apparent reality.

As we have seen, in assuming the Holoverse concept, you assume that our world view creates the reality we have come to accept; if you expect to see violence, then you are putting that expectation into the Holoverse and The Mind feeds that back to you, confirming your expectation that the world is a violent place. This happens on many levels, so depending upon what we put into the Holoverse, The Mind dictates what we get back.

If we continue to put into the Holoverse the same old story, day after day, year after year, without necessarily being conscious of doing this, we create a personal reality based upon conditions that we were taught to believe and that confirm our world view so strongly that no other possibilities exist. This creates major division between peoples which ultimately leads to conflict. Even conflict then is an affirmation that the world is as we expected it to be.

But . . . what if we no longer fed the old story into the Soup, what do you think you would get back? What would your world look like if you changed that which went into making it?

Lost in any drama it is hard to even realise that there are options. The few options that may be open to us still depend upon what is put into the Holoverse, and if you believe that bigger pebbles, rocks or bombs are going to increase your safety and comfort levels, then you are still trying to create a world based upon your apparent insecurity.

And of Course Nothing Really Changes

If we continue to assume that The Mind is indeed non-local, that the states of Omniscience, Omnipotence and Omnipresence exist in The Mind, then these states must be accessible to all the individual components of this Mind, meaning me and you.

What prevents us from realising these states? What is it that prevents us from even being aware of these states? What is it that does not allow us to recognise the benefits, the incredible power inherent in the understanding and total acceptance of these states?

According to Buddhist teachings, that which prevents us from knowing the True Nature of Mind is our Karma and our Obscurations.

Karma is a commonly accepted word, often used to describe an individual's path and the challenges the person faces, I understand this to be true, as far as it goes.

If we step back a little and observe Karma from a more objective point of view, it appears as though all actions, all thoughts, all words are the result of what went before. How can they be otherwise! All action that we take in this moment arises out of thoughts, beliefs, actions that went before.

For example, back to the person who sees the world as a violent place. This person expects the world to be a violent place. Where this belief began is not important at the moment. It is sufficient to know that this person has an expectation and that The Mind confirms this expectation.

So the individual feeds an expectation into The Mind, and The Mind confirms that the world is indeed a violent place. No judgement, remember! What choices then does the individual have but to react to the violence this person sees around all the time! Likewise for someone born in a world of apparent lack; that person has been conditioned to put this expectation of lack into The Mind, and what does The Mind give back? Lack of course.

So it has been said and believed that this feedback is the individual's Karma.

Karma can best be seen as 'charge', like the charge held in a battery. The charge itself is neither good nor bad, nor right nor wrong; it is simply charge. Once expressed, i.e. the charge in the battery has been used up, it no longer contains charge; if it is not a rechargeable battery, then it is now useless; it has no purpose.

If we understand Karma from this simple observation, we understand that Karma is charge that needs working out, releasing. Yet instead of working through it, most people seem to be lost in this Karmic Charge and instead add to it. We add to it by the energy we give to situations.

Back to the expectations of violence or lack. All the time we feed back into the system the same energy, the same results will continue to present. Because the feedback loop appears so incredibly real, it is hard to imagine that there is a loop to step out of. We have been totally sucked into the reality that we have created. So real does it appear that we go to great lengths to defend this 'reality'.

Defending our reality, in essence giving energy to an illusory state, ensures that Karma never dies. I say illusory because, as Erwin Schrödinger once commented:

> 'Every man's world picture is and always remains a construct of his mind and cannot be proved to have any other existence.'

Or the Buddha again:

> 'The objective world rises from the mind itself.'

These comments confirm the illusory nature of reality which is kept 'alive' by the energy individuals, or large groups of individuals, continue to feed into the system, The Mind.

Imagine if the collective stopped believing that violence was the answer to all their problems, or that lack was a concept that no longer existed.

Later I will explain why I believe that Karma is itself an illusion.

So Karma can come in many forms, but no matter the form it appears in, it is charge that needs to be expressed.

A quick example: My father always wanted to travel the world; however, due to life's circumstances he was not able to do this. This was a Karmic Charge that he could not express, so what happens? He passes that charge on to me. For many years I had no idea that I was working though charge that I had 'inherited' from my father. Until one day I realised that my own desire to travel the world was indeed the Karmic Charge my father was not able to express.

Coming to this understanding meant that I was able to consciously work through this charge, not adding to it but releasing it.

I have been around the world and visited more countries, lived with so many different peoples, that I no longer feel any need to travel very much at all. Possibly more to the point, the Karmic Charge of travelling the world was not passed on to my son; he is content to be a 'homebody'.

It is interesting that from a Buddhist perspective, charge, or Karma, needs to be expressed by a living body. Once we have passed from this physical reality, there is no one who can release any charge, there being no body or awareness to do so. If you have done much space Clearing, as taught by me, you will have experienced the residue of charge left in buildings or in the land or associated with furniture. A person, before passing, would have expressed charge, an emotional expression for example, without conscious awareness. Such a charge will, depending upon various environmental factors, remain in that environment until it is released.

If we fail to understand this, if we are still driven by any degree of insecurity, then it is likely that we would avoid or deny such charge existed, even assuming we were able to detect such charge. Detection of charge depends upon the sensitivity of the person experiencing the situation and/or the intensity of the charge itself. My experience (and that of many others) has been that we can release charge held in the space. The living body releases any charge, depending upon certain conditions being met.

If we keep following this line of reasoning, then it is likely we would come to the conclusion that everything, all thought, word or action, is Karmic. Our whole experience is Karmic, expressing charge that has built up. Failing to recognise this, we continue to add charge, which just increases the pressure to 'do' something to create a more comfortable existence for ourselves and those closest to us. This 'doing' just adds charge that will need to be released at some stage. Violent conflict is often the result of a charge that has been given energy, and continues to give energy to that charge until it explodes.

It can then be seen that Karma is indeed preventing us from accessing more information of a liberating nature from this Mind. All the time we continue to take personally, or identify that which we believe to be our Karma, our understanding of the world is limited to the perceptions and beliefs centred on belief patterns of the past.

Our ability to see the big picture can be likened to viewing the ceiling of the Sistine Chapel through a keyhole. We get glimpses of the magnificence but never get to see the whole of the work.

Obscurations

So what about these 'Obscurations'? What are they, and what part do they play in preventing us from seeing the big picture?

My understanding of Obscurations is that they are the filter system of the personality. These are inherited or acquired aspects that go to make up the personality of the individual. In other words the patterning that we come to believe in that makes us see the world through conditioned eyes. What we put into The Mind, the Holoverse, we get back. Putting the same information in and getting the same information back.

As Albert Einstein once said:

> 'Reality is merely an illusion,
> albeit a very persistent one.'

So persistent indeed that it is not possible, for most, to see beyond the illusion. Any number of people will try to make sense of the illusion, to try to deepen their understanding of the illusion. People are often to be found trying to solve problems within the illusion. Social media is full of people sharing their views of the illusion, failing to recognise that it is an illusion that they are discussing.

All the time we continue to take the illusion seriously, personally, we will remain unable to see the bigger picture, for we are just focused on a tiny part of the bigger picture, which of course is still an illusion.

You have to laugh at the seriousness of some.

The Buddha was reported to have said:

> 'Since everything is a product of one's own mind,
> empty of meaning like a magician's illusion,
> having nothing to do with good or bad—right or
> wrong, one may well burst out in laughter.'

Yet according to Einstein, this illusion is so strong, so persistent, that it appears impossible to break out of.

Impossible of course all the time that we think it is in actual fact reality. Our quest to understand the deeper meaning of reality, or uncover old details, continues, based upon what we currently believe. Yet as mentioned many times, what we currently believe is information that the filter system of the personality feeds into The Mind and what The Mind gives back. And of course The Mind feeds back what was put in, confirming that your original beliefs are true and valid, rather than the product of viewing the *Mona Lisa* from a distance of 5 cm through a pinhole when you see two pixels of colour and think you understand the nature of the world.

It is easy to see how the filter systems that we have inherited or acquired over time influence our perception of the world—especially as those perceptions are constantly validated by the feedback we keep getting.

So Karma and Obscurations are that which prevent us from recognising the True Nature of Mind.

Several of the quotes I share refer to the human mind. I believe that this is just a way of describing how humans understand and create their personal reality. The jury is still out on whether we have a mind or not, or if as I suspect, we access The Mind.

What does 'think about it' really mean?

The simple answer may be 'I think, therefore I am.'

But following my increasing understanding of who we are and how we fit into the bigger picture, I have my own 'thoughts' on this. Just who is it who is thinking. All the while we hold onto the belief that we are separate individuals, it must be 'me' who is thinking.

Yet as I continually discover, the 'I' is not separate from the collective. And assuming The Mind is non-local and we are all tapped into The Mind, then we see that we are a part of that which we call The Mind. We cannot be separate from this Mind.

Through many years of practicing and teaching Clearing or developing our ability to accept whatever shows up without blame or judgement, without identifying or taking personally that which shows up, it has become evident that our physiology changes the moment our focus shifts. When our focus changes, any associated phenomena we were noticing before our focus shifted fall away. The speed with which our physiology changes depends very much on how strongly we have identified with the emotions, feelings or thoughts that we held true in the past.

Back to the person who believed the world was a violent place for a moment. For years, possibly all his life in this body, he has seen the world as a violent place. This has created within, down to a cellular level and neurological level, conditions within his system whereby he goes into an immediate reaction when these old patterns are triggered. He has, unconsciously, invested a lot of time and energy into his belief—primarily because of the nature of the Holoverse, which has fed back to him that which he put in, constantly affirming his point of view, namely that the world is a violent place.

As a result of this constant reminder of the state of the world, his system now reacts very strongly so that every time there is a trigger, an environmental condition or just that he expects to see violence, violence is in fact what he sees. Now everywhere he goes, he sees violence, which leaves no doubt in his mind that the world is indeed a violent place.

For him to effectively change focus would be a challenge, as his body's default is now violence. For someone who has come to expect the world to be an anxious place, again depending upon how much time and energy have been devoted to this point of view in the past, this is going to determine how quickly one can change focus. For someone who has come to expect the world to be a quiet place, a beautiful place, then less energy is required to get them to change their focus.

With a change of focus we change the chemicals, the amino acids, that cascade through the body. If violence is our conditioned reaction, then amino acids that we associate with violence dominate our internal reality. If anxiety has been a major part of our lives, then the particular amino acids cascading through the body would be associated with anxiety, and so it goes.

Any particular reaction, no matter what it is we react to, is going to create the amino acids associated with the dominant emotion. It is a very powerful feedback loop that keeps us a prisoner to old ways of thinking.

Back to who is thinking. If we are a part of the non-local Mind, we access information contained in this great field of information. The information that we access depends upon where we focus our attention. Where we focus our attention depends upon past conditioning, or our Karma and Obscurations and the effect they have on where we are able to focus our attention.

If our past conditioning demands that we focus on violence, revenge, lack, not good enough, etc., then that is the reality we put into

The Soup, The Holoverse, The Field, The Mind of God, name it what you will, and that is the reality that we appear to live in. This is a very convincing reality because this is the world you see and live in on a daily basis; no other options exist, according, that is, to your perceptions and beliefs. We are and will remain victims to our past as long as we keep putting the same information in, and it appears to be a condition of the past that there are no other possibilities.

Yet the call to wake up, the cosmic alarm clock, being a part of The Mind, is ever present, always ringing; yet we are unable to hear it because we are so addicted to the past, there is no room in our awareness for anything other than surviving within the self-created reality that is our constant companion.

Any sudden wake-up to a different reality, coming from a place where you have invested heavily in the old ways, may well lead to a psychotic episode; the sudden shift, a shift that shatters your old perceptions of reality, may be too much to handle, too much information in too short a space of time. It has happened to some in the past, not too many fortunately, for this sudden breakdown of that which we considered reality may well lead to being rejected by the society which you once belonged to. The collective has many ways to deal with those who do not fit into the commonly accepted roles.

Who can say if this opening up to a very different reality is sudden though. None of us really know the journey of the other; we barely understand our own journey outside of past conditioning. So if a person has been walking this path for many years/lifetimes, then awakening will be just another step on that journey, only appearing sudden to those still lost in their own drama.

The Buddha was reported to have said:

>'Follow this path for three lifetimes
>and your awakening is guaranteed.'

Three lifetimes! Well if you thought this was your first rodeo, then you are very much mistaken. Perhaps not 'your' as in who you believe yourself to be now; rather that it is the charge 'you' carry that has been reducing in line with your increasing awareness.

We still haven't finished with who is doing the thinking. Currently it is assumed that 'you' are the thinker. Go back for a moment and consider that you exist within the bigger Mind. Your conditioning determines where your focus goes, and your focus determines your reality. Any conversations you have with 'yourself' happen within the greater Mind. So thoughts are determined by what went before. I would not recommend trying to go back to where this all started. The Mind, what you understand to be 'your' mind, is just not capable of seeing the bigger picture; it can only relate from within 'your' currently manifesting reality.

I imagine it is a little like tunnel vision; we only see what we expect to see. Much of what is written about in this book may go against popular thinking; yet this is what 'I' am seeing. I am not seeing more by focussing my awareness on any particular subject; rather what I am developing is a lack of focus. Admittedly I have, for many years, had an interest in the teachings of the Buddha and so been inclined to a more spiritual approach to life. Then the question arises, why? Why would I, a Westerner, be interested in such things? I may know a little of the why, but that thinking is based upon what I currently understand of the way life, human life, works on this planet. Not the full picture by any stretch of the imagination.

And as my current thinking is so different to what it was a few short years ago and radically different to what it was years before that, I make no claim to this being the final word in my understanding. As my path develops, my understanding of that path changes. Not quite on a daily basis but pretty rapidly nonetheless. I guess this is one reason I continue to follow this path, I never get to the point where I know it all. It is unlike many vocations where repetition over many years takes you to a point where you no longer have to think much about what it is you are doing; it comes automatically because of your training.

To comprehend my current way of seeing the world, best read all the book before making your own decisions about my sanity. Remember looking at the ceiling of the Sistine Chapel through a keyhole? I am not asking you to believe any of this; yet if you have read this far, you must have an interest, or at the very least a mind that is open to exploring new possibilities.

Still trying to work out who is doing the thinking? What is a thought? We know, from personal experience, that an emotion is something we feel in the body, so there must be a physiological component to an emotion—more of that later as well. We also know, from personal experience, that a physical feeling, pain?, is also felt in the body, and we understand that this is the nervous system of the body reacting to trauma, slight or severe.

But a thought? Nothing physical about a thought. At least not as far as my awareness goes there isn't. We may begin to understand the process that happens in the brain when a particular signal is received, some external stimulation, maybe even as a memory, triggered by external phenomena.

Nikola Tesla once said:

> 'If you want to find the secrets of the universe,
> think in terms of energy, frequency and vibration.'

Something I am beginning to understand more and more. Assuming that The Mind is pure energy—and non-local—having no form, consisting of all the frequencies possible and vibrating at various rates, then it must contain all information, past, present and future. Depending upon the particular frequency or the amount of energy put into that specific frequency, we, being a part of that Mind, interpret those frequencies through our own rather unique filter system as 'reality'.

As Albert Einstein once said:

'We are slowed down sound and light waves, a walking bundle of frequencies tuned into the Cosmos (The Mind—my words).

We are souls dressed up in sacred biochemical garments and our bodies are the instruments through which our souls play their music.'

Then it is not so difficult to accept that our individual systems are in constant relationship with The Mind, interacting, receiving and giving back information.

The world, as we perceive it, according to Tesla and I am sure many others, consists of energy, frequency and vibrations. It is our rather unique nervous system that is interpreting this information into shape, form, colour, sound, etc. If you had the nervous system of a dolphin, or a moth, or an ant, then the world would be a very different place. The same world just perceived through a different, unique nervous system.

Then a thought must consist of the same information but is interpreted differently to physical feelings. Maybe it is another aspect of the brain that can produce signals; those signals coming from the brain are not always of a frequency that results in physical feelings but of something very different which we call a thought. In our, often very limited, range of awareness, we have given names to the various aspects of life. We call a certain chemical, when it is allowed to enter the body, a feeling, emotional or physical, a name. Pain, anger, frustration, pleasure, etc. The more emotive the name, the more intense the feeling.

Being tuned into the Cosmos, or The Mind—the same thing—we receive certain signals. The signals that we receive appear to be dependant upon where our main focus lies at any point during the day.

Our focus is a product of the past, what we have been taught, what we have come to believe. So access to the vast storehouse of knowledge that is The Mind is controlled by our past, or rather any attachment, addiction, we have to that past.

So the thinker, as I suspect, is the soul interpreting the Cosmos through the developed personality based upon their education and personal experiences. If that education has convinced the individual that the feelings are theirs, that the thoughts are theirs, then of course we can expect the soul, through the personality, to believe that they are the thinker. Once sending that thought out into the Holoverse—read Cosmos, Mind, Field, Quantum Soup, whatever—and that thought is returned and supported by the vast majority of other personalities currently on the planet, then the thought that I am the thinker, these are my thoughts, my feelings, is constantly reinforced.

You, whoever you think you are, may have trained yourself to look at certain areas of the Cosmos, Mind, etc. and got the feedback, often what you were looking for, sometimes surprised by the feedback you get. Yet if the information in The Mind is vast and unlimited, without end, a great storehouse of knowledge, past, present and future, then your search is just uncovering a tiny part of the information contained in The Mind but misses the bigger picture. That being that all information is available to you, but your search, your attempts to understand the nature of the world you live in, is limited by the very search parameters you have employed to understand The Mind.

I think (?) that it is very exciting, this journey to understand The Mind through the many avenues open to us; mine is just one of many avenues, though instead of maintaining a tight focus, I have chosen (?), for whatever reason, to let my vision go out of focus, no longer getting attached to any one point of view, any one channel of research.

From this understanding you are the thinker, but only because that is what you believe. Your belief that you are the thinker has been fed back to you by The Mind, based upon the energy you have put into

The Mind. All the time you put in the same energy, the same results will be returned, continually reinforcing the idea that you are the thinker, that the thoughts are yours.

Change what you put in, change what you get back. This is a popular subject for the increasing number of self-help workshops available. When we see that what we are putting into The Mind is a combination of that part of the self we are aware and accepting of and the Shadow, the parts that we are not yet aware of and have not yet accepted, we can see why any wish or desire that we put into the Soup doesn't yield the results we wished for.

In our ignorance of the major part the Shadow plays in creating the reality in which we find ourselves, this constant sabotage undermines any attempt to change our lives.

Recognising this and beginning to take action is the first real step we can take to reach the Death-Less State, although there are many benefits other than the Death-Less State to be had along the way. I doubt that the Death-Less State is something most people consider, and even if you did see this as the ultimate goal of this journey, you will have to wonder why it is so important. Surely a life on Earth is sufficient; why would we want whatever this Death-Less State offers?

This can be a short-sighted view that is a product of limited awareness, of the belief that there is nothing beyond this life. Remember, if this is the belief you feed into The Mind, then the feedback will confirm this. Doesn't make it true though. Maybe truth is just a perception seen through the eyes of a discriminating mind.

How can an observer, looking at the ceiling of the Sistine Chapel through a keyhole, realise the true beauty of the complete painting?

How can anyone with limited, narrowly focussed awareness understand the true nature and complexity, the vastness of The Mind?

We do not even have to be open to wanting, needing, even realising that there is such a state. The Death-Less one. Although that may be the ultimate goal of all beings on the planet, it can be so far removed from your 'bucket list' that you are not even conscious such a state exists, or if it does, what is so important about it.

Forgetting about the ultimate goal, if indeed that is what it is, and focusing on the present should be enough of an incentive to create a better life on planet Earth. In my earlier years I was aware of this place (?) called Nirvana, a place of what exactly, I had no idea, but it sounded good. I read about the journey of Gautama Siddhartha, later to become the Buddha, the Awakened One, and his subsequent teachings, but I understood almost nothing. Just words holding certain ideals that really held only a promise of another state. What that state was I had no concept. So you could say, with regards to these teachings, I was truly ignorant, just a spark somewhere in the depth of 'my' mind, for in those days I still thought I had one, a mind!

I have read a few books that planted seeds, but those seeds were going to need a lot of nurturing before any understanding came of them. So my limited understanding was more like something in the background of my awareness, a voice if you like, guiding me, prompting me towards certain people, certain situations, certain understandings. Not that there were any voices in my head. Just a few pointers that presented certain options. Was I free to choose whether or not to follow these 'options'? I don't think so.

Unfinished Business

We are all on a path, either a path of our own making or a path that has been created by our subconscious conditioning. Whether we realise we are on a path or not is another product of the subconscious. In earlier years I did sense that there were aspects of my life that were indeed Karmic, and eventually I came to understand that I was releasing some charge, charge that had been handed down to me by my father. It was only much later that I began to see that all aspects of my life were Karmic; i.e. charge being expressed to be either released, where I was conscious (semiconscious!) of those charges, or added to, where I remained unconscious, the Shadow at play there. Obviously while I remained unaware of the charge stored in the Shadow, or as I like to call it my cosmic backpack, this was not recognised or accepted, so remained very much in control of the journey and that which showed up on that journey.

It was such an opportunity that presented after I had returned to Australia from overseas travels/adventures. I bought myself one of the original Apple computers and set myself up as a desktop publisher after being asked to design, lay out, and prepare for print a book a friend had written.

This was a big learning curve for me and opened up many new possibilities, many of which are still useful today. During the course of this business, I was asked to prepare some promotional material for a client, and this opened my eyes to another possibility. This new possibility was an approach to working with energies of the environment, restoring greater balance and harmony where people suspected that their personal environment was causing problems for them or their family. I read the course presenter's prospectus as I went about the work of producing his brochures and came to a deal, a swap, my time for a course, one evening a week for 10 weeks.

I still recall coming home from the first evening of the course and being so excited by the information that had been shared. I remained awake for hours talking about it. This, as you may imagine, was the beginning of a very new journey for me. The point of my sharing this story with you is to help you understand how situations present along our path that lead us in certain directions, towards certain goals, each of which may appear random or isolated but which in fact are a continuum, an unfolding based upon what we had previously put into the Holoverse. (Consciously or otherwise!)

Gradually this new business took over from the desktop publishing, and I became very busy working for many clients around Australia, although not in the way we had been taught. This is an important part to our story of a search for the Death-Less State. Not that it was realised as such at the time. At the time it was just an interesting way to create an income; only later did my eyes begin to open to a different understanding of the world and the part we play in it.

It became obvious to me, early in my days as a consultant and 'Clearer of environmental energies', that my very presence in an environment was what was changing the energy of the space; it had nothing to do with what I might do to bring about a change. This was confirmed by the feedback I continually got from clients. So with no personal understanding of what was happening, it was obvious, to those I worked for, that there was indeed significant change in the energy of the home, so much so that through word of mouth of satisfied clients, my own work grew quickly.

I came to realise, over time, that if I was making a difference to the energy of the space simply by showing up, being open to notice whatever energies were likely causing the clients to invite me into their home, then we were all doing it, making a difference. To some degree or other, each of us was partly responsible for creating the energetic environment in which we lived. It was then that I expanded my practice from just Clearing the space to Clearing the person as well. This was a complex process at first, primarily because I still felt the need to 'do' something to help the other.

However, if we each contribute to the creation of the energies in our home, why would people create an environment that was uncomfortable? I can only think of one reason, the Shadow, the cosmic backpack that we all carry. The Shadow aspects of the self are running their own program in the background and are responsible for creating that which we consider uncomfortable in our lives or our home. For most, the first thing we do when we notice areas of the home that make us feel less than comfortable is to blame these unseen energies. As we do in other areas of our life, if someone makes us feel unhappy, angry, weak, etc., we 'blame' the other.

Yet for me, this tiny realisation that I could make a positive difference to the energy of an environment, that I could have an effect on these unseen energies, was big enough in itself, but to recognise that we are all doing it, all the time, was the true eye opener.

The more Shadow that existed in any one person's backpack, the more likely it was that they were going to create situations in their home that they found uncomfortable. Without being aware of it, they had created a situation that reflected their Shadow. All of us, when confronted with aspects in life that make us feel uncomfortable, tend to blame something, someone, some situation. The more I noticed this, the more obvious it became to me that while we remain unaware of the effects this Shadow has upon our lives, the more we remain a victim to circumstance; it certainly appears that way.

In one of Jung's comments on this Shadow, he said that while we fail to recognise the Shadow and its effects upon us, we will call that which shows up in our lives fate. Yet this is simply not true; it is not fate if it is something of our own making, if it is something that we can change. But how to change it? This is a fundamental question that we should all be asking ourselves instead of bemoaning our 'fate'. What can we do about it?

Well very little it seems, for all the while we see our problems arising from an external source, failing to recognise the part we play in creating those circumstances, we will remain a victim to our 'fate'.

I have found a way—well not strictly true; maybe a way has found me, or did it simply show up on my path because of the unconscious pebbles I have been throwing into the pond? Everything arises out of past actions; it just doesn't show up, at random, on your doorstep.

So it is all a part of the great unfolding that is my life. I wasn't not looking for 'a way'. I was not looking to be an author, to be a person who could help others, to be a teacher of this information. I was not consciously looking for much at all, just a simple life, earning an honest living, living a peaceful, happy life. Hah! And yet here I am. Well I do have a happy and peaceful life, so that is something I guess.

Back to the evolving path of a Clearer of energies. When I realised that we each play a part in creating the space we live in, our very being, much of which was outside of any conscious control, was impacting our environment, then I expanded my consultancy to include personal Clearing, for what use was there in Clearing the energy of space if we did not work on what was possibly the fundamental cause of the problem, the individual(s) living in the space.

I think one of the most powerful effects this process had on me, however, was what was happening to me, to my understanding, as I worked with the space or the people in the space.

To clear, according to my evolving understanding, one must first be clear. Because as I have come to see, it is not about something that I 'do' but as a result of something that I 'am'.

So to whatever degree 'I' am someone who can embrace the frequency(ies) of any particular disturbance in the house, I can collapse that specific charge. The more frequencies that I open up to, recognising that the effects experienced by 'my' body are just conditioned reactions to various stimuli but do not in fact 'belong' to me, I can be more objective about them and therefore not blame, judge or personalise the feelings that I experience.

Whether in the early years of my practice I understood this way of being or not, this was exactly what was happening and the reason why my clients felt at peace in their homes. Because I had, unknowingly, collapsed the charge that was held in the environment by my presence and my opening up to the energies that appeared to be out of balance.

What this unconsciously led to was an opening of my heart. Where before I had taken personally whatever I felt—remember me, mine, you, yours—now I was able to recognise a feeling, not judge it, attach no blame to it and certainly not identify with it. If I were to give it any energy, that would mean adding to the charge and not releasing it. This did not happen overnight but was a slow process made possible by the many environments and individuals that I opened my system/body to experience. The more we open, with awareness, the more frequencies we learn to embrace, even those frequency patterns held in our own Shadow.

Collapsing Our Shadow

Without realising it I was collapsing the energy of my own Shadow.

Without realising it I was becoming more compassionate, for a heart that does not blame, does not judge, does not personalise must, as a result, become more fearless. No longer afraid of my own Shadow, the heart opened more, creating a more compassionate awareness. A compassionate heart is still throwing pebbles into the pond, but instead of pebbles of fear and anger, blame, judgement, revenge, poverty, they were pebbles of compassion. What do you think is going to come back to you? What sort of reality are you helping to create if these are the pebbles you throw into the pond?

At the time I had no idea what was happening or why, in part because I was not noticing any feelings in my body as I explored the energy of the space, nor of course did I notice any change as a result of my 'work'. It was only the feedback from clients that kept me going; after all, if they noticed a difference, something must be changing even though I did not know what.

This led to working towards discovering what was happening. I realised that in order for me, or anyone, to feel anything, we needed to feel safe with what we were opening up to. It seemed that safe or not, I was making a difference.

The more I developed this practice of Clearing, the safer I became, because repeating the mantra time and time again that this was not my feeling, simply how the body has been conditioned to notice, I gradually became more comfortable with a broader range of feelings.

I was able to judge less, attach no blame and certainly not personalise or identify in any way with the feelings I was noticing, because by now I was noticing a lot. Apparently, for most of us, the safer you feel, the more you feel.

This served many purposes. One was that I was able to give more immediate feedback to my clients, often supporting the very same feelings they experienced in the space. Perhaps more importantly though was what this process was doing to my body, specifically my Shadow.

Even though I was not consciously focussed on any of my Shadow, how could I if I were not conscious of any Shadow aspects in the first place, with them being in the subconscious. This accepting of many varied frequencies was beginning to reduce any charge still held in the Shadow. Remember Tesla: *'Think in terms of . . . frequency . . .'* So information stored in the Shadow/backpack is stored as specific frequencies; frequencies equals information equals experiences that we are not comfortable with or aware of.

So in a roundabout way I was working Clearing my Shadow without being aware that was what I was doing.

So What Was It Gautama Siddhartha Was Looking For?

Obviously it took him a few years to find it. But how did he know this state existed, whatever it was. He had, first, to work through his Shadow, and for sure he had one; otherwise it would not have taken years to reach his goal. His Shadow may have been different to most, being born a prince and kept away from general society. This must have created a certain personality. A personality that he needed to work through without recognising what it was that he was working through.

Same as me! And likely all beings on this planet.

At least I could reference his teachings to give me some support along the way. If the stories about his life, his journey, are correct, that he was prompted into this journey by witnessing old age, sickness and death, then he went through extremes to find this Death-Less State until he realised that the extremes did not give the answer he was looking for, and what was that answer? What was he looking for? Apparently he was looking for something beyond the suffering he saw after he left the palace.

Working through the extremes, mortification of the flesh, denial of all comfort after a life of comfort, allowing the pendulum of his life to swing between these opposites, he searched for an answer. Recognizing that this was not working for him and then allowing the pendulum of his life to settle, swinging neither one way nor the other, he settled on the path of the middle way, realising that neither extreme held the answer.

I have not had to go through such extremes because of the candle he held that lit the way, I was already aware of the middle way so did not need to repeat his journey.

But our journeys did/do have something in common. When we began, whenever that was, this journey, we believed that in order to find the truth (?), we had to work through layers of misunderstanding, like peeling an onion. We felt that if we peeled back enough layers of the onion, we would arrive at the truth. This is still a commonly held belief amongst many seekers of the truth.

We could follow this path until we get to the stage where we recognise the process, that some 'one' is working through many layers, peeling the onion, in order to come to the truth.

I suspect that we continue to follow this onion peeling until the scales tip in favour of the conscious as against the unconscious—the Shadow. When this moment occurs, we understand that there is not, nor ever was, an onion to peel. It was the addiction to the conditioned mind that was the problem; it was this habit we had become addicted to that appeared to be the onion that we had to work through when in reality the onion was a product of our own imagination.

The Web of Indra

The Hindu have a way of describing this journey that I have found very helpful. It is called the Web of Indra.

This Web of Indra consists of multi-dimensional threads of consciousness. It is said that wherever these threads meet another, i.e. cross, there is a pearl and that pearl is you.

It is also said that if a candle was lit, anywhere in this multi-dimensional state, then all the pearls would know about it immediately, their all being connected, and so transfer of information is instantaneous. Potentially this is true because we, the Clearing community (and likely others that I do not know or have no direct experience of), have experienced this. When we consciously connect to 'clear' another, no matter where in the world they are, we notice a shift in our own physiology similar to the shift the person we are Clearing feels.

We discover this later of course, unless we are in contact with them via some software over the Web. So we 'know' that something happens when we put our attention on another to whatever degree we are available or the other person feels safe with us. Clearing happens because we do not judge, blame or identify with that which we notice, to the best of our current ability. By not judging, blaming or identifying with that which we notice, many things can happen.

Primarily we allow the other to express this charge, whatever it may be, thereby allowing their system to begin to relax. A relaxed system is more able to take care of itself and possibly begin a journey of healing whatever their Shadow has created. Many factors are involved here of course, and the 'Clearer' can make no claim or promise anything; just 'holding the space' can often be enough to at least start the journey.

This is the effect we have upon the other. For the individual 'doing' the Clearing, they are accepting the information received from an apparent external source. This means that were the frequency of the information something that was held in their own Shadow, they are slowly bringing it into conscious awareness. This helps in releasing old charge, of which they were likely unaware they even held.

So this is just one example of the communication happening on this Web of Indra. There are many others. We can say that this Web is another way of describing The Mind, or the Cosmic Soup or God, whatever. Since the Web is claimed to be multi-dimensional, it must expand into many areas or aspects of our life (lives). The candle spoken of earlier must then represent information that is available to every being on this Web; every pearl has access to this information. Our Clearing has demonstrated this on a very small scale.

Yet for most of us currently on the planet, this does not appear to be the case. Why is this? Well I suspect partly because we have not considered this a possibility. We have therefore not focussed any of our awareness on this subject, which, as we have discovered in our exploration of the Holoverse, means that we have not been fed back any confirmation, or otherwise, of the existence of this concept. No putting in, no getting back!

Yet does this make this untrue, simply because we have not given it any attention in the past? Does anything that we have not given attention to in the past remain untrue because it has not been a part of our own experience? Is the only truth that which we have been given confirmation of? Is the truth of another any less true just because we have seen it though our own conditioned eyes and judged it as not being of value?

Is then everything true? Or nothing? Well possibly, but truth is very often limited to the eyes of the one getting feedback. My truth is more true than your truth! Really? It seems to me that all the time we see the world through our conditioned eyes, we only see a very small part of the bigger picture, whether we have chosen that or it is what our past conditioning, and thus what we have put into the Holoverse, has created.

We might well say these varied views of the world create the diversity of life on this planet, True enough, but when any individual or various groups of individuals believe their truth to be the only one and begin killing those with a different point of view, then I think we have taken the idea of diversity too far.

So what is it that is preventing us from knowing when the last candle was lit? Not really accurate because I believe the candle was always lit, the information always there and available. Yet still we only perceive a tiny point of light, if that, based upon where our focus has been.

Now we come back to the Buddhist belief that which prevents us from recognising the True Nature of Mind, aka the Death-Less State, is, in this part of the discussion, our Obscurations.

To my way of thinking, these Obscurations and the many layers of personality that we have either inherited or acquired along the way have formed a shell, or like the onion, many layers of beliefs based on our Karma or early childhood conditioning.

It is this veil, this filter system that we call our personality and to which we strongly associate and identify with, that filters out the information the candle is sharing. It also keeps our own light hidden from others.

Imagine that within the pearl that exists on the Web of Indra, that represents you, is another candle, for we are all ultimately beings of light dressed up in biochemical garments (Albert Einstein). Then the light that we are is just as hidden from others as we hide ourselves from the Big Candle in the sky. Not that we are doing this on purpose. The little light from the Big Candle that we allow in is often related purely to that which we have put into the Holoverse, so we cannot expect much to come back that does not fit into our already conditioned view of the world.

This does not change the fact that the greater field of information exists; it is just as though we have developed tunnel vision. All the time we hold onto the point of view that our way is the right way, we will continue to justify killing others so that our point of view can be safe, dominate, be more powerful, whatever. This whole process is based upon the principles that the Buddha believed this world was built upon, namely Greed, Fear and Ignorance. Take a look around and tell me this is not true!

Just about everyone I 'work' with has the fundamental issue of insecurity out of which a multitude of symptoms arise. This insecurity may well have its roots in Greed, Fear or Ignorance. This insecurity is a product of looking at the world through the keyhole, not seeing or understanding the bigger picture. All the while we continue to see the world this way, only getting a tiny part of the bigger picture, we will continue to live in fear to some degree or other. All the time we are in fear, of what? Then we will continue to try to do something to counteract that fear, which often means enacting violence, to some degree or other, on those holding different beliefs.

Is This the Definition of Madness?

I have come to these conclusions, not by reading anything or listening to anyone, for I have long ago stopped believing a word anyone told me. The reason I do not believe anyone? Well if they are sharing their current understandings and those understanding are a product of their own veils —their own filter systems—do they really know what they are talking about, or are they just trying to convince me that their (limited) view of the world is the right one? I listen but do not take seriously that which I hear.

Instead I have found that by following the path of Clearing, I am increasingly able to accept more of whatever shows up on my path. This is achieved by recognising where changes in feeling come from, understanding why they happen and knowing that they are just how the body has been conditioned to react. By practicing this we become less judgemental, less blameful, and we begin to take less seriously that which we notice.

So, inadvertently, I have slowly embraced the Shadow, brought hidden aspects of the self into consciousness where they no longer have control over my future.

Assume for the moment that all we are is what we think we are. What we think we are is a product of a past over which we had little or no control. If we practice this, then we can see that we are the personality, a system of various judgements and association with very specific phenomena. So we are just a gathering together of many points of view. This is the veil through which we see the world; this is the information that we feed into the Holoverse. Of course this then returns to us, which further justifies our association with the points of view which make up our personality.

So we have a very strong connection to the personality, something that we did not choose, something that we did not agree to, something that we were/are not fully conscious of.

Our personality then is made up of likes and dislikes, rights and wrongs. It is a compilation of those aspects of the self we have embraced, or accepted, and the Shadow aspects, those parts of the self that we are not aware of. If we believe all of this to be who we are, what happens when you bring some of the Shadow into the light? However we do this is immaterial at this moment. Can you even imagine what is happening to your perceptions when you do this?

Back to the Web of Indra. Imagine this multi-dimensional Web of energy lines; at the junction of any crossing is a pearl, which contains a candle, which is you. Now because of when and where we were born, there are certain patterns of information that we either inherit via genetics or acquire due to our familial or social environments. As we have no choice at this stage, we take all these conditions and beliefs personally, and they become the personality through which we see the world.

This 'personality' also acts as the filter system which determines what we see and why. When the filter system is so strong, the light from the candle is diluted, even polluted by our expectations. Expectations that arise because of the conditioning we went through as a small child. Now we do not even know a candle, a light, information, exists because we can no longer see it; if we do see any of the light from the candle, it is through the filter system of the personality, which distorts it to fit our expectations.

Hardly surprising then if we misunderstand the nature of the candle.

In turn this filter system that we call our personality is also blocking out the light that we are from others, so those others just see the personality, not the inner light. Remember the other is also looking through their own filter system, judging what they see as either fitting in with their expectations or conflicting with them.

The nature of the Web of Indra is that all pearls are connected and information transfer between the pearls is instantaneous—think 'entanglement', a state where separation only appears to exist but in actual fact all particles, read 'pearls', are connected because they are all, in reality, one.

When we clear, a space or another person, we are opening up to how our body responds or reacts to the energy of the other. By noticing change in our physiology and being able to ascribe that change to the energy transmission of the other, we are able to be more objective about that particular feeling, also read 'frequency'. As we become better able to accept a broader range of frequencies without taking them personally, we are slowly peeling away layers of the onion, the personality or the filter system that we had previously so strongly identified with.

Imagine then that the filter system gradually breaks down. Slowly so as not to cause distress to the inhabitant of the body.

As the filter system weakens so more of the light of the candle can get in, likewise more of the light that you are can get out.

This is where any understanding that I now have has come from. As mentioned earlier it did not come from reading books or listening to others; it came directly from the candle. The information storehouse that is The Mind. The filter system, as it weakens, allows more light/information in. With this growing understanding comes a greater awareness of what exactly you are feeding into the Holoverse.

Another effect of acceptance is that the Shadow gradually loses any intensity it had, thereby lessening any control it had over your journey. A natural effect of a reducing Shadow is less pebbles of insecurity, judgement or blame, or association with any one belief pattern, get thrown into the pond, into the Holoverse. The less conflicting pebbles thrown into the pond mean the less conflict comes back.

Now there is less conflict that comes back, conflict which may previously have caused us to throw even bigger pebbles into the pond in order to help us feel safe, valued, or override the pebbles that others had thrown into the pond, based upon their beliefs which apparently opposed ours. When conflict is not returned, we no longer need to protect our points of view, so we no longer throw pebbles into the pond in defence of our own insecurity.

When your Shadow is no longer in control of what you throw into the pond, then you can be much more conscious of what you do throw into the pond. With a growing opening up to the light of the candle which equates to a lessening of association with personality, there comes into awareness a different state of being. The self that we thought we were begins to fall away. Without a strong attachment to that self, which really only consisted of points of view, comes the realisation that the Shadow was not yours. It was never yours; that Karma is not yours, was never yours. It was only the strong attachments we had to the body, the thoughts and feelings that gave the impression that the Karma was ours, that we had a Shadow.

Full Circle

If we continue to follow this reasoning, then there is no one to throw pebbles into the pond. We are the pond, have always been the pond. We just forgot it for a brief moment in time when we thought we were a body and the associated thoughts and feelings.

However, if we continue to hold onto the personality, the filter system, and we continue our struggle to create a safe world in which we can live, even if it means that there is no end to the struggle, it will go on and on, passed down through generations, all holding onto the same points of view, all seeing the world through their unique filter system.

Heaven and Hell

This holding on leads us into the states the Buddhists call the Bardos, or Realms of Becoming.

I think that believers in heaven and hell are thinking in the right direction but have simplified it down to the two extremes. It is that same thinking that tells us that one is where the good people go; the other is for the bad people. Following this thinking there has to be someone who decides whether you deserve to go up or down.

What if there is no arbiter, no guardian at the gates? What if it is our actions that decide where we go? What if it is the charge that we have yet to discharge that determines where we go after the body dies?

I have spoken about charge, possibly called Karma, needing to be expressed and not added to. To understand the Bardos and what creates and sustains them, we need to take a side trip on our path toward the Death-Less State.

To do this we should allow for possibilities that we may not have considered before, or even been aware of. If we have never entertained the possibility that we have an emotional body or a mental body, it doesn't mean that they do not exist; it is simply that we have never thrown the question into the Holoverse with a relatively open mind. It is the same for all possibilities that we do not accept. The information is there, in the Holoverse, The Mind, if we were to go looking for it. We need to be looking without pre-established, inherited judgements.

It has been my experience that we have an emotional body, sometimes called the astral body, and a mental, or causal, body.

These are energetic fields that arise as a result of being in human form, having a body. They are not visible, obviously, because the frequencies that make up these 'bodies' are of a vibration that is too high for us to see. Yet with a little training, it is possible to 'feel' or 'sense' them.

I have found the emotional body to contain information about all the emotional memories that we have experienced. When there is a particularly strong charge held in this emotional body, a charge that has not been understood or still retains significant intensity, then it will have an impact on the physical body, causing all sorts of issues. Without recognising this as being possible, we look for answers to those issues in the material world, not so helpful if we continue to deny the cause of the imbalance, or issue, that we are working with.

This is just an aside to any cause leading to a Bardo State. This is an important aside without doubt, but it is a valuable step towards understanding the next field—the mental or causal body. This is said to hold information about who we have been, who we currently believe ourselves to be and who we will become. Going back for a moment to the emotional body and any stress held in that energy field, if the stress was caused by a misunderstanding or trauma in our distant past, then a belief, rightly or wrongly held about any situation in our past, may have caused an extreme emotional reaction.

This reaction may well have originated as a result of a particular belief held in the mental field, which subsequently caused trauma to be held in the emotional body. Simplified, if we hold a particular belief—in the mental field—then if that belief is challenged, it may well lead to an emotional response, which creates a shift in our physiology, which we take personally.

Accepting this for a moment, we can see how our thoughts, be they conscious or still held in the subconscious, shape our personal reality. Where we put our attention gives rise to the creation, on a physical level, of our personal reality. Remember, pebbles into the pond.

Now we can see how that charge, often held in the body as a result of a particular way of thinking, can build, creating pressure in the system. When the flow of energy in any system is blocked, pressure builds. That system may be mechanical or electrical, or our body; when the pressure build-up exceeds the tolerances built into the system, the safety valves, then the pressure will find the weakest point in that system and cause a malfunction of the system.

The human body is no different in this respect from a mechanical or electrical system. With the human body, that build-up of pressure may cause an angry or violent outburst; it may also cause an internal breakdown, burnout, panic attacks, significant health issues. It has become my experience that stress build-up is responsible, in a major way, for premature ageing. So best to avoid any build-up of stress in the body. Most do not realise that stress is building in the body until the warning signs become really obvious, so obvious that we can no longer deny them.

This build-up of charge does not always result in angry or violent expressions, burnout, panic attacks, etc. It can simply be a build-up of a desire for more of something. If that desire is never fully realised and released, then it may well be that charge that determines where 'you' go after the body dies.

The 'you' in this case is the soul. When the body dies with unresolved charge, then the charge seems to take over. Without a body there is no way to relate to the physical world. You need a nervous system to interact with the physical world; you need the ability to discriminate between light and dark, hot and cold. Without these abilities, all associated with a body and its unique nervous system, you have no way of relating. You become a victim to any charge that remains.

If there is sufficient charge held in the mental or causal body, then that is what determines where you, the soul, goes after the body dies. No one sits in judgement. Can you imagine such a job, being in charge of that department, the department that determines where you go? A major bureaucratic nightmare! And then there are all the subdepartments which arise dependant upon the beliefs of the individual at the moment of death. Easier to let the charge that you still hold decide. And that decision is not black or white, up or down, heaven or hell, but many shades and levels in between.

So the Bardo is a personal choice. Not that the individual is capable of choice at that stage of their never-ending journey. Maybe, like a department store, there are many areas, each devoted to a particular charge, and then subdivisions within those departments each based upon intensity of charge.

Where there is a really strong association with the body, the thoughts and feelings, and that body dies suddenly or violently, then the mental field may well create another body, for whatever reason, often shock, to allow the soul to work out charge. But again, no body, no ability to work out any charge. This may be the state of limbo, or purgatory, stuck in no-man's, or -woman's, -land with no control over where you go or how, or why.

If as the Buddhists claim, charge needs to be released by a living being, then once the body is no more and charge remains, then that soul may well get stuck, until someone comes along, notices charge held in the environment and through conscious awareness releases that charge on behalf of the deceased. Or depending upon the intensity of the charge, a certain amount of 'time' needs to pass before the charge can collapse, or said charge is passed on to another body for them to work out. Confusing, sure.

There is a Buddhist practice called Phowa, which is the transference of consciousness from the dying person to a trained practitioner. This supposedly, depending upon various levels of ability, takes charge from the dying person, thus affecting any following Bardo States that person moves into.

Now we get closer to the reason why reaching this Death-Less State can be of value.

To the degree that charge is held, desire is unfulfilled or pressure has not been released, the individual will find themselves waking up in a Bardo of their own creation. Yet there is no longer a discriminating mind to evaluate the situation. The soul may find itself in heaven or hell or any state between those opposites but without any real ability to recognise this, to 'do' anything about it. There is no capacity to view the manifesting reality, Bardo, with any degree at all of objectivity. So, basically, there is 'no one' to wake up, let alone realise 'they' are in one of these Bardo States.

We, according to charge that has arisen out of identification with the body, are victims of that charge. Much the same as we are while alive, in the body. For while the Shadow continues to play a major part in creating the world we live in, we will remain a victim to circumstance without any true control of our destiny. We may believe that we are in control, but any control that we think we have is a product of our conditioned past. It is not really control in that we are not able to choose freely between all possibilities. Rather decisions made while under the influence of these Shadow aspects have created realities where choices, or options, become more and more limited.

We 'think' we have a choice, but that choice may be between B and C. What happened to the rest of the alphabet? Why can we not choose W or X or Y or Z? Many reasons. I suspect they just don't appear as options because the 'decisions' we made in the past precluded these options. Remember it was the effect of the Shadow that caused us to follow a certain path, not free will. Free will may well arise when the Shadow is no longer in control.

This may become more relevant when later we question why some are born into times of conflict, famine or other less desirable realities than others.

If we die with the Shadow still playing a significant role in the unfolding of our life, and our death, then whatever degree of control we thought we had while we were alive is no more. This assumes, following some Buddhist teachings, that there is a part of who we are that survives the physical death process—a soul? Or is it a degree of consciousness that survives?

So a major part of this search for the Death-Less State would be bringing the Shadow into the light. In Jung's words 'making the darkness conscious'.

All the time we fail to recognise this Shadow and the effects it has upon our lives, we will remain a victim to it. It appears, whether we understand it or not, that we are playing a part in the script we were handed. Is this what our lives are all about? To take the part we have been handed seriously, to deliver an Oscar-winning performance? It may be that the part we play has written into it an awareness that we are just playing a part, that the part is not who we are. It is more than likely that the part we are playing doesn't have that awareness written into the script. We would then be totally lost in the part.

What determines the part we play? Who is handing out the scripts? Well, quite possibly, according to when and where you are born, into what circumstances and what background, we may find an answer. Someone brought up in a different reality will have a different answer, a different understanding and relationship to the world. We may well believe that our answer is the right one, the only one, the best one. Conflict will inevitably follow this approach to life as it meets others with very different points of view.

Accept, for the moment, that these Bardos are a part of the soul's journey; you may refer to them as heaven and hell, though I think that is too simplistic. I would maintain that it is not so black and white, but many shades of grey in between—all sorts of states exist according to this understanding. If we can accept that it is the stored energy, or charge, that has not been recognised or released during our time in the body that determines where we 'go' after the body dies, we can see how this could unfold. Of course it is no longer 'us' that goes anywhere, for there is no 'us'; if there is no body, no discerning mind, then surely there can be no 'one' who goes anywhere. No 'one' as we currently relate to ourselves, identifying with the body, the thoughts and the feelings as being 'ours', who 'we are'.

If this is the case, then there can be no 'one' who gets into heaven or hell. Are heaven and hell just concepts that have been repeated through the ages as a means to control? The ultimate carrot and the stick? Or are they self-created 'realities', the two extremes of the Bardo State? States that are dependant on and created by the actions and beliefs of the individual who took the part they played while alive so seriously that they forgot they were just playing a part?

Following this line of reasoning, then heaven and hell are just Bardo States. States that are reflections of the charge, conscious and unconscious, that the person held onto during life and continue after the body died. We are still playing the part after the body dies. The 'we' here would have to be either the soul, still lost in the part they were given, or due to a strong attachment to the body. This 'continuity' often manifests as desire, still wanting more. More sunrises, more chocolate! More coffee, alcohol, sex, drugs or rock and roll. It really doesn't matter what 'more' we want. If the desire is still strong, in other words the desire, or charge held, has not been fully released, then nothing changes after the body dies. The desire, or charge, carries on.

Then the 'soul' will be taken wherever the desire leads. The mental, or causal, body will re-create the appearance of a physical form, obviously just an illusory state which then experiences life in the particular Bardo the desire, charge, has created. Dependant upon the amount of charges associated with this desire, there will be no understanding of what is happening, no discriminating mind that notices the passing of time nor is able to recognise what is happening.

If what the Buddhists claim, that charge or desire, same thing really, needs to be expressed or released by a physical form, then after death any charge/desire that remains must 'take over' and determine where the soul goes. I see no problem accepting this. How can someone who no longer has a body, no longer with a discriminating mind, no longer having any control whatsoever over their future, release charge other than through the creation of a state that we currently refer to as a Bardo?

Without a body we can create no more charge, nor can we release charge. Like a small sailboat without anyone steering it, we are at the mercy of the winds and tides. If we are blown onto rocks, it is because we have no control over where our sailboat goes, If we are blown into a great, empty ocean, if we are blown into a metropolis, a tropical paradise, a never-ending line of drinks on a bar, the charge will take us where it will.

I suspect that if our next step involves being taken, because of desire or charge, into a Bardo State, then rebirth is inevitable. It might take minutes, it might take millennia, not that the soul in the Bardo will be able to tell time passing. No discriminating mind, remember? No concept of time as we, in a physical body, in a physical realm, know it. This physical world we currently inhabit is one of subject-object, one where time matters. With no body, no discriminating mind, time cannot exist because there is no 'one' to observe its passing.

The intensity of any remaining charge, or desire, seems to be the determining factor of where the soul goes and how long (?) it spends there. Also what determines when or where or into what circumstances the soul will be reborn?

Death may be likened to falling asleep and waking up in a Bardo State, a state that you do not recognise as being any different from your waking life in a body. Depending upon charge, and any expectations you held in life, the movie will appear to continue. Expectations are an important part of the process.

Return, for a moment, to the Holoverse and that which you put into the pond is always coming back to you. Based upon your expectations, which are based on all previous experiences that keep showing up on your path simply because you expect them to, then you will be truly caught up in those expectations.

This strong identification with expectations guarantees that you will continue to experience life as it appeared yesterday. Expectations are in no way related to any fundamental truth other than what you, by your addiction to process, give it. I do not think this addiction, especially as though in all likelihood the addiction is a result of a subconscious process, can simply fall away at the moment of death.

I have heard it said that some Buddhists believe this reality that we currently inhabit is also a Bardo State. Hmmm. Think about that for a while—your current state, the part you are now playing, has arisen out of past thoughts and actions. It is reasonably easy to see how our current thoughts create the world we live in. Think of an unpleasant experience, an old, or recent, memory. Do you notice how the physiology of the body changes? Now think of a pleasant experience. Does the physiology change? We can very quickly, and with practice, change the physiology of the body. If your attention, your focus, no longer dwells on a painful past, then the feelings associated with that painful past will gradually fall away. You are no longer feeding pain and discomfort.

Life Is a Continuing Unfolding

Understanding this we can see how 'life' is a continuum, no beginning, no end, just an ongoing unfolding.

If we no longer give energy to a negative past, then that past ceases to be. It may remain as a faint memory but will no longer have any control over your future. Not so easy for many, as the seriousness their part demands precludes any other options than to take seriously the part they have been handed. Even this seriousness has to be the product of the past. It cannot arise out of nothing. There has to be some cause creating an effect. Continued identification with the part just means that the reality you currently experience will not change.

I have also heard that the moment of death is the greatest opportunity to realise an enlightened state. I believe that is possible. I also believe that it is unlikely if the desire or charge is so strong at the moment of death that we 'miss' the opportunity. It is the continued identification with the part we play, the seriousness with which we play the part, again determined by thoughts or actions in the past, that prevents us from realising the opportunity.

It is the degree to which we still identify strongly with the body, with our thoughts and feelings, that determines how quickly, and into what state, we fall when we die.

When I sleep, as in a regular nightly occurrence, nothing special or spiritual, I am not aware of anything. I do not, to my awareness, dream. Nothing exists when I sleep. Not so the case for many others of course. But for me, this is what happens, or doesn't happen!

Now the 'fact' that I have no memory of anything happening while I sleep doesn't mean that nothing happens. I am just not aware of it.

This can best be demonstrated by the following story: For many of my early years, I was very impatient; yet I never realised this, all the time so lost in impatience that I could never be truly objective about this state. So I was an impatient person without realising I was impatient. No possibility of subject-object, so lost was I in that particular drama. Associated with this inability to notice the feeling of impatience was a general inability to feel much at all. I believe we are all feeling all the time; we just fail to recognise feelings for a variety of reasons.

I did not notice feelings because feelings were too uncomfortable. I was not safe, because of my past, getting in touch with 'my' feelings. Hardly surprising then that I did not notice feelings, in the body, of impatience, or much of anything else. As a by-product of my work as a consultant Clearing the energy of homes and people, I became, over time, more comfortable noticing feelings. This happened through the process of acceptance, meaning I was feeling safe enough to notice feelings. I was able to accept more because I knew, through my work, whenever I connected to the energy of space, that the feelings I was beginning to notice only arose as a result of my connecting to various energies in the environment. The feelings themselves were not mine; I was just the observer. Developing this observer status allowed me to accept more and more feelings without taking them personally.

Slowly I became aware of the feeling of impatience as it began to arise in my body. I noticed the feelings before I got lost in impatience.

Noticing before getting lost in impatience was the key. I then had a choice, whereas previously there was not choice; it was impatience immediately.

My choice then was either to give in to the feeling of impatience, which meant giving energy to it so that the physiology of the body changed and I 'became' more impatient, or to say to myself, this is the feeling of impatience—what's next? And thereby cutting off the supply of chemicals that I associated with impatience. No more chemical production, no more feelings of impatience!

So for many years I was a victim to impatience without being aware of it. I may now be a victim to an experience while I am asleep without being aware of it. Lack of awareness does not mean that something is not happening; it simply means that I am not aware of it happening.

The same applies to the Bardo States, if we do currently inhabit a Bardo State, and my/our present situation in life is simply charge working itself out; then the best I/we can do, given the script I was/we were was 'given', would be to consciously release as much charge as I am/we are able. When I understand that my current reality is indeed the result of charge or attachment to the past, or old expectations of life, then I may be encouraged to make a conscious effort to change the thinking. I have learnt that we do this by the practice of acceptance, not by going into battle with the self (which accepts the manifesting reality as real and then tries to 'do' something about it).

My 'liberation' from any subconscious charge around impatience is just one of the many benefits that I personally have experienced. We do not need to be even aware of the possibility of any Death-Less State to begin walking along this path; it does not have to be an intentional goal that I work towards. Understanding may, or may not, show up along the way.

If we accept that we get back in life what we put in and that a lot of what we put in is the result of any Shadow aspects of the self that remain hidden from us but co-creating our world, then in truth we can no longer blame others for any undesirable situations we may encounter. Others may appear to confirm our own beliefs and judgements, but this is only because we have yet to fully understand the part we play in creating those situations.

If everyone on the planet believes that others are responsible for their challenges, then nothing will change because everyone still puts the same information into the pond that they did yesterday, and the day before, and the days before that. How can any manifesting reality change when the thinking that created it remains the same?

When, through a process of conscious acceptance, our Shadow is brought into the light slowly, we free ourselves from any subconscious process that created the world we live in. We reduce the state of victim consciousness that our Shadow had created.

One of the results of this is that we meet less resistance along the way, less conflict and less challenging situations. This can be called 'going with the flow', where manifesting that which we are is effortless. This may take some practice because we are not the only person throwing pebbles into the pond. We may have made a conscious effort to be more aware of the part we are playing in creating our world, what pebbles we are throwing into the pond. Yet if there may still be situations where we judge the actions of others, remember we live in this pond along with every other member of the human race, most of whom are still throwing pebbles into the pond creating their own waves, their own realities. These waves surround us, making it difficult to sort out what is ours, what is the others. It also appears difficult if not impossible to not judge or blame the actions of others that do not fit into our world view of right and wrong, good and bad.

When we begin any practice of acceptance, people will ask 'how do I know what is mine and what is the others?' If we assume, for a moment, that nothing is mine and that it only appears to be mine, it only appears to be mine because 'I' have identified with a feeling. For example, for much of the past, I have given so much energy to a specific thought or emotion, that I have created a very specific response/reaction in my brain, meaning every time circumstance triggers this response/reaction, the same chemicals are produced in the brain, creating the same internal changes, which, as it has happened this way for so long, we automatically identify with that thought or feeling.

If we go back far enough in time, in this individual's journey though life, we will see that at some point that which we feel so strongly about, that which we identify so strongly with, was never a part of us. It became a part of us due to circumstance, a particular way of thinking, a result of the values we have either inherited or acquired due to when and where we were born. Essentially wherever and to whatever we have given energy, or identified with a thought or emotion, created the illusion that 'this' is ours. Even when and where you were born was not the result of a lottery; it was dependant upon what went before.

As an example, if while in a body that was born into a very religious time and family, you came to also believe strongly in that religion. Every aspect of your life—because of the particular pebbles associated with your religious beliefs that you threw into the pond, your beliefs—was confirmed on a daily basis, creating an even stronger identification with your inherited beliefs.

For many this connection to their religion is so strong that it survives the death of the body. The next 'reality' that this soul experiences, the next Bardo State, will be heavily influenced by the charge, around religion, that the person held while in a body. Dependant upon any other charge this person still held at the moment of death, the Bardo will be influenced, not by any external power, but by the remains of charge held by the individual.

Now when the time comes for this soul to reincarnate, it will be drawn to an environment, family, time and place that support the energy that is yet to be released. In all probability it will be born into another religious family, further enhancing the belief of the individual in the religion of the family. Following this line of reasoning, we can see how whatever it is that we believe in strongly enough is going to play a major part in who we now believe ourselves to be.

In our search to understand where various beliefs may come from, we could go back to the birth of the body. This really will not lead to any answers, as it doesn't go back far enough to be able to see where the belief came from. We question current thinking from a very personal point of view, which, by its very nature, is limited.

At some point when there is no body to experience life as we know it, is there still a religion? If there is no longer a subject-object situation, any self-created reality based upon past experiences is not real in the sense it is not something happening in this physical reality; rather it is a projection, an expectation of the soul.

An important aspect of the Death-Less State is the realisation that we are not limited to the body, that we are not the thoughts (just the thinker!), that we are not the emotions (just a soul experiencing emotions). Yet what is the soul? Is it a part of that which we now call The Mind? Is it The Mind or a separate aspect of The Mind? If it appears separate, is that because the soul is still identifying with the body, its charges and desires, even after death. If the attachment and identification with the body survive death of the physical, then is it not reasonable to assume that the soul creates another reality, just a continuation of what it was doing in life. This is the other reality that the Buddhists call a Bardo—a Realm of Becoming!

All the time that we hold onto the belief that we are the body, our beliefs in who we are, within the body, get stronger because we continue to put energy into those old beliefs and values.

The Buddhists say that when we are born into this physical world, we literally lose our minds. We forget our true nature, the connection we have, always, to The Mind. Does this mean that before birth we were fully integrated into The Mind?

Because of the process of being born into a body, into a state of separation, we forget our true nature as we take on the persona of the young child. This appears to be a necessary part of the journey of the soul. Otherwise what purpose is there to being incarnated in a physical body?

What if, before birth, we were not, for whatever reason, living in total connection with The Mind? We fail to recognise that we are an aspect of The Mind after the body dies. This may happen because we still hold onto the belief, held before the body died, that we are an individual soul; that we were an individual perpetuated by our 'time' in the Bardo that we most recently inhabited, the nature of the Bardo being a reflection of charge and desire we held in life. If this is the case, then we never truly lost our mind in the process of being born, again because we never really remembered, or recognised, the true nature of mind because when the body died, we fell asleep and awoke in a Bardo. We mistook this Bardo for reality because we had nothing to compare it to, no longer having a body with a discriminating mind!

So the wheel keeps turning. All situations arising out of past situations, it is only our addiction to the past that creates the present, with the manifesting present reinforcing our beliefs, and so it goes.

So the benefits arise from being in the flow of energy, where all things arise seemingly effortlessly, a state achieved by practicing non-judgement, i.e. acceptance of what is. A common misbelief, amongst many, is that if we accept things as they appear to be, without taking sides, without judging one aspect as good, the other as bad, we will allow 'the other' to win, to gain power over us. So instead of accepting, we fight back, throwing more pebbles into the pond. All this does of course is to reaffirm your current insecurity and lack of awareness of what throwing pebbles into the pond really achieves. A continued state of separation and the resulting conflict that follows.

Now if being in the flow meant that you were no longer a victim to your past, no longer sabotaged by the Shadow, it may well mean that you were starting to get back real choice. Not the choice between A, B and C that previously determined the world we lived in, but choices of A through Z.

An example: Many years ago I caught a cold that developed into a terrible cough, a cough that just would not ease up. We had been planning on visiting South America at the time, but health reasons, and common sense, told us this was not the way to move forward. Instead we made a short trip to Holland to visit friends. While staying at our friends' house, on the first night I think it was, the coughing became so extreme that I broke, or fractured, a rib.

If this has ever happened to you, you will know how painful that can be, especially knowing that when you next cough (or laugh), that pain is going to be intense. My friend arranged a visit to her doctor for me the following morning.

A wonderful man, who, after the usual check-up, arranged for me to get an X-ray. Off to the hospital I went, still in a lot of pain! The result of the X-ray came back. Nothing about a broken rib! But they did notice a dark spot on the lung, which turned out to be pneumonia, treatable with antibiotics. The story doesn't end there.

The X-ray also showed a Shadow behind the dark spot that was the pneumonia. Of course alarm bells went off, and the doctor wanted me to go to see a lung specialist. Understanding what he was concerned about, we decided to sleep on any decision. In the morning we made the decision—we were going to Mexico, not back to the hospital or any specialist. Once on that slippery slope, once putting yourself in the hands of people with their own expectations, the choices become very limited. A, B or C!

I 'chose' to not go down that expected path. I did assure the doctor that I would get an X-ray once in Mexico, which I duly did. The only comment that came out of that visit was 'Did you know you had a broken rib?' Well! That was the reason for the original visit, the pain from the broken/cracked rib.

This X-ray showed no trace of pneumonia, nor ominous dark Shadows; all was perfectly clear. Now it may be that the Shadow was nothing important, but giving in to fear would have given energy to the

Shadow. Visiting a doctor who specialised in finding whatever it was they were looking for was going to be a big pebble in the pond heading down the road to cancer. Choosing a different path, as a result of opening up an awareness to other possibilities, other ways of thinking, led not to cancer but no cancer.

A year later I had another X-ray as I began coughing again. Still nothing there, just a topical infection, easily fixed. So our choices dictate our future. Remember, nothing arises out of nothing; everything arises out of past actions, ways of thinking. I do pay attention to physical warning signs, as long as I notice them early enough to change direction. Leaving or ignoring, or more likely simply not noticing, the warning signs until you really have developed an issue in the body often then means choices are getting fewer and fewer until medical intervention is needed.

Another example of following this path, whether it leads to the Death-Less State or not, is not as important as the many benefits that arise on the way. If you no longer throw confusing or angry stones into the pond, you no longer meet confusing or angry people or situations.

This was described in a most elegant way by the Greek poet Constantine Cavafy in his poem 'Ithaca'. I have quoted this in other books, and it bears repeating, for no matter how many times you hear it, each time a 'different' person hears it. Each time they understand it a little more. The opening verse goes like this:

> 'When you set out on your journey to Ithaca, pray that the road is long, full of adventure, full of knowledge.
> The Lestrygonians and the Cyclops, the angry Poseidon—do not fear them:
> You will never find such as these on your path, if your thoughts remain lofty, if a fine emotion touches your spirit and your body.

> The Lestrygonians and the Cyclops, the fierce Poseidon you will never encounter, if you do not carry them within your soul, if your soul does not set them up before you.'

Because of his Greek heritage, Cavafy used traditional Greek demons, Lestrygonians, Cyclops and Poseidon, which in our understanding become our personal demons. Not necessarily demons as in scary creatures of the night, but demons like anger, impatience, frustration, blame—the list goes on.

According to the poem, if we hold these within our soul, we will continue to meet them on the road. *The Holographic Universe*, by Michael Talbot, had not been written when Cavafy wrote this in 1911, but the whole process of creating our personal reality is the same, according to the poem and the Holoverse.

Keep throwing pebbles of anger, impatience, frustration or blame into the pond, and you will keep meeting them along your way. Stop, or begin by reducing the number of these pebbles you throw into the pond, and you will stop meeting these along the road. They will still exist, simply because there are a lot of people still throwing such pebbles into the pond, all creating the world in which they live. You will no longer meet these people or the situations they represent because they are no longer a part of you; these Shadow aspects have been brought into the light of consciousness.

This is another of the benefits of which Jung seemed to be perfectly aware. Your path becomes much more peaceful; situations that required a lot of energy to 'deal with' or 'overcome' no longer arise, so less stress builds up in the body; less time, energy, even money is required to maintain a state where you feel safe or valued. This is because your unfolding reality is based more on compassion, which you have gained through greater understanding, which you have gained by a developed practice of acceptance, which you have gained by taking the first step into non-judgement.

When the pebbles thrown into the pond are pebbles of compassion, then what will you meet on the road? Compassion of course. The pond is not judging you, simply feeding back what you put it.

Now if you are not putting stressful pebbles into the pond, you will get back a much more peaceful state. This can easily be seen as a less stressed body, and a less stressed body is less likely to get sick; a less stressed body will notice any imbalance before it becomes a problem, thus avoiding the problem by stopping giving energy to it before the problem manifests. A less stressed body, i.e. a body that no longer identifies with stressful pebbles, will stop putting them into the pond. It becomes a process that grows, not by what you do or what pebbles you throw into the pond, but by what you don't do, the pebbles you no longer throw into the pond.

As your system relaxes as a result of what pebbles you no longer throw into the pond, you will no longer encounter those Lestrygonians, Cyclops, Poseidons. 'You' get out of your own way—those aspects of personality that created problems fade into mere memories of a past life. In this way the body can begin to heal itself if we are not feeding contradictory information into it. For example, if you still get very angry, your brain, which may well be producing the chemicals which later become known as anger in your body, is not judging your actions; it is simply doing what it is told. You may not be in charge of this process mainly because there are still Shadow aspects for you to deal with. It matters not to the brain. It will continue to produce the chemicals associated with anger; it does what it is told!

Those tiny chemicals of anger are transformed into amino acids, which then enter the cell, thus causing the emotion that we call anger to present in the body. 'We' identify with anger. All this means is that by taking the feeling personally, we are instructing the brain to produce more of these chemicals, thereby intensifying the feeling of anger in the body. The more intense the feeling becomes, the more likely we are to take it personally, believing it to be 'our' anger. Remember though that these angry feelings are quite toxic in the body; they are going to cause problems later in life as the system gets overloaded with the chemicals of anger. Other functions of the body are reduced in their efficiency. That's because we override the body's ability to stay healthy by continually feeding it a diet of anger, or anxiety, or impatience, or . . .

This is obvious when the little light of understanding goes on; until then we remain a victim to circumstance that appears to be beyond our control. Or as Jung said, when we are unable to recognise our Shadow, when we are unable to bring it into consciousness, then what we meet is our 'fate'. Our 'fate' is simply what we meet along the road, and what we meet is determined by what we put into the pond.

A big challenge for most when they begin to walk this path, from ignorance into awareness, is what they meet on the road which seemingly has nothing to do with them at all. This can be overwhelming if that person has not developed a new way of looking at and dealing with what shows up.

The two major players in what shows up are what we and the rest of humanity have put into the pond. Often it is so long ago we forgot we put it into the pond, or more likely our Shadow put it there without any conscious participation on our part. So we did not know what pebbles we were throwing into the pond. We just get the feedback from the pond. Feedback that we take seriously, personally, and we react by throwing another pebble, consciously or not, into the pond. You can see how this becomes a self-perpetuating reality.

As noted above, the other player is the rest of humanity. Simply because we begin a journey to reduce the number of angry pebbles into the pond does not mean that everyone else does the same. They are still throwing angry pebbles into the pond, the repercussions of which we observe. If we still associate in any way with the information that the pond feeds back, we will notice the anger and we will react to it; we do this by throwing our own angry pebbles into the pond. Maybe our reaction to anger is not anger; maybe it is fear, or anxiety (another degree of fear!). Then our reaction, be it conscious or subconscious, perpetuates the drama.

As we develop our practice, which slowly grows as a result of becoming more aware, then we may well notice a lot more than our partly closed system did in the past. Partly closed because, due to past circumstances, we did not feel safe experiencing certain energies. Not feeling safe limits what we feel to a range within which we do feel safe and comfortable.

This may include but would not be limited to physical feelings. If we are not feeling safe with certain energies, certain frequencies, then we will not notice them. Not noticing them does equate to not having them. While we feel the need to protect ourselves from these frequencies without awareness, we slowly build up charge in the body until it becomes clear that there is a problem. When a problem manifests, our options, or choices, are limited by our past actions, in this case our insecurity. An insecurity that was driven by a fear based on misunderstanding of information. So if that which arises in the body came about because of fear or misunderstanding, from a state of insecurity, the belief that allowed that to come to pass is now in control of the choices available. A, B or C. Not D, E or F or . . .

Stop Running Away

So past beliefs and decisions limit the options when a problem appears. Were we more conscious of what was going on in the body, a situation that arises out of the opposite of fear, then the problem that manifests in the body may well have never come to pass, thereby never needing anything to be done about it.

These are some of the overwhelming forces that seem to confront us when we stop running away from our past, while we are developing the process of acceptance.

The more we practice, the less we meet along the road. I do see though that in the early stages a lot more appears on our path, much of which we have no recollection of ordering. Whether we ordered it or not or it is an order placed by another ultimately doesn't matter.

The goal is to treat all orders the same. When those in their early days along this path ask me, 'How do I know what is mine and what belongs to the other,' my reply is, 'None of it is yours.' For many this is just a temporary understanding that helps them develop greater objectivity around that which they notice. Although I do believe that ultimately whatever they notice is not theirs, they may believe it to be theirs simply by past association with the thought or feeling. But this doesn't mean it is or ever was theirs. Simply something that they have identified with in the past, and continued to identify with, giving it energy. We do this to the point where the thought or emotion appears quite intense. The more intense, the more likely we are to identify with it. Intensity is not an indication of ownership, just something you have given a lot of energy to in the past.

It may appear to be real, depending upon the amount of energy this thought, this feeling, this belief pattern, has been given in the past, not just by you but by all those who believe the same way. So the more people giving energy to any belief, the more 'real' it appears to be. The more real it appears to be, the more people we will get discussing various points of the manifesting reality, as though whatever point they are talking about is real, rather than a product of many people believing in this in the first place. Quite interesting when you stop for a moment and think about it.

So depending upon the number of people believing in your point of view, the more real it appears to be. The more real it appears to be, the more people will give it energy. The more people giving any belief energy, the more real it appears to be.

Now if you are so far down the rabbit hole the drama has become very real, then there is a great fear that if you stop adding your pebbles of retaliation into the pond, the other will not stop and you and your ideas will be defeated. Because we have devoted so much time and energy to what we believe to be our personal reality in the past, then a huge charge has built up around that perception. We then see no option other than to continue to throw those same pebbles into the pond. Thus aggravating an already unstable condition.

From this perspective there is no chance that either party will stop throwing stones, come to their senses and realise what has created the current situation.

Fortunately I do not believe that any party to conflict can, nor needs to, stop adding to the flames of conflict. Apart from the fact that we are all on a road and appear to have to work it out for ourselves, we need to find a real way out of the chaos that our lack of awareness, of understanding, has created; the charge that has built upon between different sides of any conflict, be it a one-on-one relationship or between nations or religions, has to be expressed or understood on another level.

However, understanding that ultimately we are all a part of the same consciousness, no matter what point of view or value judgements we hold, then nothing is 'mine' in the sense that there is no longer an individual 'I' to make such a claim. This understanding arises the more we bring our 'own' Shadow into awareness, As mentioned earlier, if we are what we have believed ourselves to be in the past, an isolated, separate individual, then this belief has been reinforced by the feedback we get from the pond.

When, through accident or design, we reduce the pebbles of conflict we throw into the pond, then less conflict returns. One of the effects of this, as explained earlier, is to reduce the density of the filter system through which we view the world. Reducing the density allows more light, more information held in The Mind to enter our awareness. As the effectiveness of an intense filter system begins to fall away, the sense that 'I' am separate reduces. Obviously when this reduces, the awareness that we are all connected, all a part of the one, all a part of The Mind arises. As we become more conscious that we are all a part of the same consciousness, it becomes increasingly impossible to blame the other for any challenges or problems that we face.

Alongside this growing awareness, we recognise, through our own journey, that the Shadow only exists to the degree we continue identifying as a separate, isolated individual. Another significant effect of the practice of acceptance is the growing understanding that we are not isolated individuals but a part of the whole. A part where there is much less of the 'me' and the 'mine, the 'you' and the 'yours'.

Your own Shadow falls away because you have brought it into the light of consciousness, and in the process you have stopped blaming or judging others. This causes your own Shadow to weaken, allowing more light from The Mind to enter your awareness, which just increases the light/information available from The Mind.

Then there comes a point where you realise that Shadow only existed to the degree you identified with the body, the thoughts and emotions. The logical conclusion is that Shadow was never personal.

If this is the case for you, as you have discovered as a result of walking this path, then the same must apply to all beings. They may not have realised it yet, but that is not a prerequisite for change.

With your understanding and your compassion, another product of acceptance, you stand at the edge of the pond and notice all the information coming back to you, currently amplified by social media. Now instead of reacting to it as you may have done in the past, again with or without your conscious participation, you no longer add to the charge by throwing in your own judgemental thoughts or emotions. Like and dislike, agree or not, it is all the same. It will not appear to be all the same to another if they are still in judgement of that which they notice coming back to them from the result of past actions.

Here I am reminded of a quote attributed to Erwin Schrödinger:

> 'Every man's world picture is and always remains
> a construct of his mind and cannot be proved
> to have any other existence.'

As we now appear to exist in a chaotic world, a world gone mad with its desire for an individual or group of individuals to feel safe at whatever cost to its fellow human beings, it is easy to feel overwhelmed and feel powerless to 'do' anything to change it. If we remember that we, by no longer giving energy to that which presents in our life, can reduce the conflict that we experience, we see, as a part of our awakening journey, that the charge that reaches us all, as inhabitants of the pond, is simply that, charge seeking to express itself.

While we take the charge personally, we just add to it. Creating more chaos, conflict and confusion. When we develop the ability to simply notice this charge without reacting, then we effectively collapse the charge in 'our' compassionate heart. Although it is no longer seen as 'our' heart, we just stop adding to the charge, thereby reducing it.

We do this with no help from others who are still taking the charge seriously. The collapsing of the charge has now become effortless for us, because there is no longer any judgement about the charge. It just is information that we no longer carry any personal preference around; it is no longer a part of who we believe ourselves to be. As mentioned a little earlier, this is an impossible task for someone still lost down the rabbit hole, but is something that no longer requires thought or effort on the part of the soul that has reached the point of not judging, not blaming, not identifying with all the phenomena that it previously took seriously.

This allowing of all information to collapse may well be similar to what Gautama experienced in the evening just prior to his enlightenment, his awakening, his being named the Buddha.

According to the story, and I am not able to quote it word for word, but just to give you the concept: As Gautama Siddhartha resolved to not move, to not come out of a deep meditative state until he had broken through the barrier that appeared to exist, that prevented his enlightenment, he sat beneath the Bodhi tree in quiet contemplation. It was then that Mara, the god of illusion, sent the armies of hell, the feasts and the famines, the plagues and the pestilences, the dancing girls (or boys!) to tempt Gautama out of this meditative state by generating a reaction in his body to all the phenomena placed before him. Unshaken, unmoved by any of the illusions Mara presented, Gautama became the Buddha.

Imagine this in the language used in this book. Gautama sits by the pond, quietly observing all that arises, all that comes back from the millions of stones thrown into the pond, and remains unmoved by any of it, simply collapsing the illusory nature of the phenomena. Once he had collapsed it all by not giving energy to any of it, his eyes were opened to his true nature.

This could well describe our own journey towards the Death-Less State. We begin by exploring both extremes of life, not necessarily in the same body; it may take a while for each of us, souls, to find the middle way, the path of least resistance. When we do, and according to the teachings, it is inevitable that, at some point (three lifetimes it has been said), we will awaken. The awakening will then allow us to pass through death without falling asleep. Retaining consciousness through the process, we will have access to all that went before, to all that lies ahead, assuming we still identify with past, present and future!

Don't set your eyes on the goal, for the goal is just an ideal. It means nothing without direct experience, a personal knowing. Instead focus on your daily life as it appears to be now. If you have heard the wake-up call and paid attention, then your journey has evolved and you will continue to meet the supporting cast in this play of yours along the way.

With each step, baby ones at first to be sure, the light, the information, increases; it becomes clearer. At this stage it may still be energy given to an illusion. For the last part of the journey, not worth worrying about at the moment for it will come when you are ready, is the letting go of any identification with the body, the thoughts or feelings. Having walked the path to the point where you can collapse the illusion, not giving in to any aspect of desire, of fear, of rejection, then the final step is a foregone conclusion. Imagine that happening now. Lost as we are in our current reality, it is not possible to imagine it. We are so strongly attached to the body, to the thoughts, to the illusion, that it is inconceivable to imagine any other way of being.

It is my experience that not many people are aware of this path or have any interest in following it. The majority of 'westerners' on the planet, I do not know much about other ethnicities, seem to be much more focussed on getting more. More money, happiness, power, love, whatever. There are plenty of programs around the world designed to offer the chance to get more. Now if you believe in these programs, instead of working harder, itself a trap, you just need to manifest more.

I believe that the only people this appears to work for are those involved in sharing their beliefs on the subject. The majority may attend workshops, may get caught in the hype, go home full of positive intentions and thoughts of manifestation but end up in the same place they were before.

If you have got this far through this book, it should be becoming obvious that you get back what you put in. It doesn't take any effort to 'put in'; you do this automatically. Recall though that if the Shadow has not been recognised and addressed, brought into the light of conscious awareness, then it is still a part of that which you put in. It is often the Shadow aspects that sabotage any efforts you may make to 'get more'.

It is also the Shadow that generates the desire for more. A paradox. Driven by deeply subconscious insecurities, lack, not having enough, which would be primarily Karmic Charge as often mentioned earlier in the book, we are caught more and more in the belief that our reality is 'real'.

Lost in that drama, which is what we have become, through experience to feed into the Holoverse, we keep getting confirmation that more of whatever will solve all our problems. Patently untrue of course. By going deeper into the illusion that is your manifesting reality, you are simply giving it more energy, reinforcing the illusion.

Chasing goals is not a bad thing, trying to better oneself is not a bad thing, as long as you remember that you are in this world but not of this world. Meaning enjoy the journey but don't get hung up on it as being the only show in town. Try to maintain an awareness of the reality behind the curtain.

Expecting to be able manifest whatever one's heart desires without addressing the Shadow is doomed to failure. What needs to be taken into account here is the history of the individual. It is hard to tell how long one has been on the path of acceptance, nor what Shadow exists in the individual. So one person may be able to manifest everything they want because past decisions have now allowed that possibility. Who knows how long it took that individual to reach that stage. I would love to have a magic wand I could wave over those on the path, release them from their past, help them open their eyes and be able to manifest whatever they wanted.

Alas, I have not graduated to the advanced practitioner of magic yet.

The paradox is that while there is Shadow, there is perceived lack, and we have to 'do' a lot to achieve a little. That familiar Zen saying:

> 'Do a lot achieve a little—Do a little achieve a lot—
> Do nothing achieve everything.'

The only reason we have to 'do' anything is a result of the Shadow. We are in a constant battle with the Shadow, meaning a constant battle with ourselves. Strange eh! That we are our own worst enemy and yet we fail to realise that.

So while we have a strong attachment to the body, the thoughts and feelings, the Shadow also exists, playing a major part in the creation of our personal reality. This leads to an insecure outlook on life, always feeling that more will solve our problems. So we go to manifestation workshops in the hope that we will find the answers there.

Yet this apparent need for more is driven by the shadow, or subconscious desires based on insecurity.

As we develop a practice of acceptance, the attachment to the self, or more accurately the attachment to aspects of our personality, the personality, that which we believe ourselves to be, begins to lose some of its power. This will also mean that those parts of the Shadow are slowly being brought into the light of conscious awareness.

The more the Shadow aspects are brought into consciousness, the less part they play controlling our future. The less control they have, the less insecurity arises or operates behind the scenes creating symptoms of insecurity. The less insecure we become, the more in the greater flow we become.

Remember that in order to accept, we have practiced being less judgemental. Then through our becoming less judgemental, we put less pebbles of judgement into the pond. The obvious effect of this is to get less conflict back that was previously associated with the judgemental pebbles we threw. So the feedback supplied by the Holoverse changes. Life becomes easier, being more in the flow, which means less conflicting pebbles (the result of the Shadow) are thrown into the pond, and this whole process becomes easier, just because the new feedback supports this new way of being.

As this process unfolds, with less symptoms of insecurity showing up as a result of different pebbles, then the perceived need for more reduces. Not because you do not need or deserve more but because your needs are met simply by being in the flow, which means the Shadow is no longer contributing so much to your unfolding path. So by getting out of your own way, you are no longer your own worst enemy; you no longer need more in order to feel safe.

Then more will simply come to you, effortlessly. Manifestation is 'real'; it is a 'law of the universe'. It was just that your Shadow sabotaged all your efforts, making you work harder, go to more workshops, in the never-ending struggle with the self.

Remember, you will always get back what you put into the Holoverse. The Holoverse is not judging you, not deciding who deserves what; it simply reflects back to the individual that which they put in. Put in insecurity or lack, what do you expect will come back?

If there is any truth to what I have written, then moving forward it is not about saving others until we have saved the self.

While we try to help others while still lost in the dream, we are simply applying techniques, that while they may work, have very limited long-term effects. For if we think we can help another while still suffering from our own Shadow, then are we really helping?

I have chosen, because of personal experience, to not believe a word anyone tells me. I listen, but having heard so many people try to sell me an idea, a belief, I cannot support those ideas or beliefs if they lead me further down the rabbit hole.

The process of Clearing, or acceptance, that I have followed, even though it is at first just another belief, is, I realise, a belief that has been designed to self-destruct. Once, by applying the principle of acceptance to all phenomena, the Shadow has become fully accepted or released, there is no longer anything to 'clear' or accept. The training is to develop a practice of acceptance that, once this has been achieved completely, then there is nothing remaining to be judged.

Simply put, as we develop our practice, our eyes begin to open wider; we see more, we understand more. The more we see, the more we understand, the less we judge. The less we judge, the less stones of conflict are thrown into the pond. So that which the pond replies with is no longer so strongly polarised into like and don't, good or bad. The polarities are concepts that only arise in the first place because we were still throwing judgemental pebbles into the pond.

Nothing is simple, or does it just appear that way? We use the words 'cultural identity' to describe our past, our attachment to that past and the power that past has over us. This assumes that the person identifying with that cultural identity was in fact a part of that historical line. This might get confusing; it is not an easy area to describe in a few words.

Consider this: We now believe The Mind to be non-local—meaning it is not confined to time and space, meaning from our physical perspective it has no beginning nor an end. Time, as we know it, doesn't exist in this Mind. If we humans are partly responsible for the information that is put into The Mind, and The Mind has no past or future, then all the information ever put in by humanity from all ages exists in The Mind.

We are that Mind, at one with it, until we are born and believe ourselves to be separate. We are born into a world that holds certain beliefs, certain values, a world that identifies with a past, a cultural identity. Now if the person, the soul, born into a world with strong cultural identity has no memory of any past incarnations, then it would be easy for them to be programmed to believe that this cultural identity is a part of who they will come to believe themselves to be. Before birth there was no separation, no cultural identity.

That association only came about because of when and where you were born. Was it an accident or fate or something else that determined when and where you were born? As an example, hypothetically speaking, my 'soul' could have spent time in the mountains of Tibet where Buddhism was a part of everyday life. At least in the more distant past. Then because of decisions made as a result of believing that was who I was, a Buddhist, then I may have had an experience in Northern India. Still following a belief in Buddhism. This is hypothetical remember. Then as a result of who knows what, I was born in England, still with this inner knowing or remembering of the Buddhist teachings.

I give no real meaning to this story for several reasons. Mainly because when I first became aware of any Buddhist philosophy, I was aged 14 and it was during a lesson in school. I asked, if we were being taught about religion, why was Buddhism not included? This was ignored by the teacher. I had no idea where that thought came from, certainly not from my ancestral genetic memories; no one in my family tree, as far as I knew, was ever interested in the teachings of the Buddha.

It must have come from somewhere though, but where?

I can only guess at possibilities. My earlier story about being born in a Buddhist country doesn't ring really true because any understanding I had in those early years, in this body, was so basic, so 'kindergarten level', that it is embarrassing to look back and think I knew anything at all about those teachings. It was, however, a significant point in my unfolding journey. From not knowing, I walked a path learning more about this path, and that which showed up along the way has been incredibly supportive. It has led me into a much greater understanding, a knowing, of the essence of the teachings of the Buddha.

I may still look back on these times with embarrassment, recognising that I still only understand a little, but I do know that I understand a whole lot more than I did, even in my recent past.

The point of this little story is that the putting in of pebbles into the pond did not begin with this life; it is a continuous process that has no beginning or end. Previous generations have put the same beliefs into the pond in a continual process that has created that which we call cultural identity. Whatever phenomena that have caused you to be born into a society with this cultural identity have created in you a cultural identity that appears real and that is a part of your history. All societies have cultural identities that they are proud of, and where that identity may be a little weak, the society will invent its own culture, to give it a greater sense of purpose.

What if it is your first time in this particular stream of consciousness? The past of that consciousness has nothing to do with you, but because of when and where you were born, you are indoctrinated into believing that this is indeed a part of your history. You identify with being from a certain country, a certain religious belief, a certain ethnicity. You are being indoctrinated into that belief system. As a result of this, you then throw your own pebbles into the pond supporting this belief, thus giving it more energy. The more energy any belief is given, the more real it appears to be. You add your energy to the cultural identity, thus ensuring it carries on for future generations. But was it ever a part of who you are, or just something that you believe for a brief moment in time?

Sometimes this cultural identity, this nationalism, can be the cause of conflict with other people who, because of where and when they were born, people with a different cultural identity to yours, appear to be in opposition to the way of life you have been indoctrinated into. However, if all we are is a collection of beliefs that are the result of all the pebbles thrown into the pond by previous generations, and these beliefs are only kept alive by those who follow blindly throwing their own pebbles in support of that reality, the result of continually affirming these beliefs is predictable. By continually affirming these beliefs, of course this strong national identity creates such a powerful—a seemingly powerful—reality that we are lost in it; we add to it, creating further divisions between others, and the 'mess' gets more intense.

The more intense the mess gets, the more we take our part seriously; the more seriously we take our part, the more energy we give it. No wonder we live in a very confusing world. So deep are we in this particular rabbit hole that the only option, for many, appears to be conflict.

If we want to change the reality we live in, then first we must begin to collapse the conflict that we see. We cannot change anything of any fundamental nature by throwing more conflict into the pond in the hope that one day peace will arise. The Holoverse doesn't work like that.

Collapsing conflict is going to be more difficult if your previous thoughts and actions, or your association and identification with 'traditional' cultural patterns, have you so strongly convinced that 'you' are right. So the more energy you have given to any belief in the past means that your next moment is simply a repeat of past thoughts and beliefs.

Imagine a pure awareness queuing up, waiting for a body to become available. You have a history, meaning you have charge that has not been expressed while you were in your last body. You eventually get to the head of the queue where your details are entered into the great computer of The Mind. The algorithm comes up with a character; you are handed a script, a time and place to make your entry and off you go. Not much time to look at the script; just enough time to bring a smile, or a grimace, to your face and then, before you know it, you are in another body.

Are you in the body of a girl or a boy, or is there some confusion in the script about what you are? You are welcomed into the third-dimensional reality, hopefully, by your parents and any siblings that might have arrived before you. You still have some vague memory of what it was like before you took on this new little form. That is a challenge because it is only the discriminating mind that could remember, or judge, the state you were in! That memory fades quickly as you get used to being stuck in a tiny body, totally dependant upon others. Those 'others' have long since forgotten they are just playing a part and, according to their script, have played the part to the best of the demands of the script.

Now begins the process of indoctrination into the cultural beliefs of the family into which you have been born. It will not take long before you are playing your part, adding to the history of the peoples you currently find yourself with. But what is this part? Why you? The 'you' not having played this part before, having no memory of what went before, if anything, transition into a believer of the past, supported by your environment and those living in that environment.

Has the part that you now play been taken over by past thoughts and emotions that have been out into the pond by those who came before you, who followed the same line of thought? Do you have any free will at all, or do you just think you do? While in a body have you ever had any control, or do you just do what the environmental conditions dictate? All the time you react to that which the Holoverse feeds back to you, you will remain a victim to the past. But if that is what the script says, then that is what you do.

Remember, your script is a product of what went before, what Karma, the great algorithm, has created for you. This will continue until there comes an opportunity in that script for you to begin to take a step back from the part you play. You start to take a look at what is happening behind the curtain. Will you follow this opportunity? Again is it free will that allows you to do this, or is it written into your script that you should do this?

The less of the past you feed into the Holoverse, the less of the struggles associated with that path will come back to you. Eventually you will be free of the past. Can you even imagine what that state will be like?

Warning! You Are Approaching the Death-Less State

Rewriting the narrative.

The question that arises out of the above warning is who exactly is it who is approaching the Death-Less State? Certainly not a personality.

I believe that it is the personality, and the attachment we have to it, that is preventing us from recognising that we are already, and always have been, a part of this Mind. If we are interested in rewriting the narrative that we experience here on Earth, then I suspect that first we must accept where we are in the here and now. A lack of acceptance of this may well be caused by the attachment to the body and personality, which in turn could be driven by any Shadow aspects we still have.

As I understand it now, the only reason we have these so-called Shadow aspects is because we are still so strongly identified with the body and personality. A paradox?

As we begin to understand and practice acceptance, then judgements have to fall away; this is, after all, what acceptance means. Though we are not able to be totally accepting because our past conditioning is so strong. Acceptance is a slow process and will only be followed if positive outcomes become evident early on in the journey. Something to make this journey worthwhile.

The interesting issue that arises as we accept what shows up and judgements reduce is that the desire for change, if driven by discontent with the current reality, also reduces. We are only discontent with the manifesting reality because of any judgements we hold. As judgements fall away, so does discontent. So the desire for change becomes less important, and it is then that a new narrative can arise.

The biggest difficulty most people face is indeed letting go of judgements; the judgemental mind would be concerned that if it lets go of its values and judgements, then it loses power in the face of opposition. This belief only arises because of attachment to old values and of seeing the world through those judgemental eyes. When judgement falls away, so does opposition. That which we fought against falls away and a new reality begins to arise.

Hard to visualise something like that. The old thinking was that if we do not fight for what we believe is right, then the other values will win. This thinking maintains a very polarised society, a self-perpetuating illusion, one in which change, of any sustainable, positive nature, is impossible.

So we are caught in what appears to be a never-ending loop. All the time we give more energy to maintain balance or support the status quo we remain a part of the problem.

Are more people waking from the dream and beginning to question this reality? Is it in any way real? If this is the case, then we may reach a 'tipping point' where the energy needed to sustain the old way of being collapses. Indeed we may be witnessing that now in these uncertain, tumultuous times. Or are the majority simply exchanging one 'reality' for another?

This would be like any other revolution that preceded it. Exchange one way of being for another. Did revolutions really change anything? On the surface, yes, but there was no fundamental change to any deeper aspects of our being.

No system likes to lose its sense of purpose, its power base, and will struggle against change, still lost in the belief that power and purpose can be achieved and are of any real value in a newly emerging reality.

A new narrative will not arise because of new dreams, principally because the 'dreamer' has not changed on any fundamental level. While insecurity, or unhappiness with the current reality, still exists and remains the driving force for change, then nothing sustainable is possible. Any change that arises from such a polarised set of values will be the result of one section of the community wanting a particular outcome where another community will want a different outcome. Ongoing conflict has to be the result of such a process.

When enough people stop feeding the drama, then the drama becomes more difficult to sustain. I do not know just how many people are needed, but if life is to continue on this planet and evolve into a greater potential, then some fundamental changes are required. Not changes brought about through the ongoing conflict of one set of values opposing another set of values.

See through the illusion. Take a look behind the curtain and know that any real change has to begin with you. Change your mind, change your heart and be a part of a new future, an evolution of consciousness.

Much of this information will not be read by those not ready to hear it. What I have shared is based on my current understanding of how we create the world we, personally, live in and how we can change that. If understood, this information will challenge all current beliefs, for in understanding comes the knowing of what the Buddhist saying means, repeating this because it takes a few times of listening to this to begin to understand it:

> 'Since everything is a product of one's own mind,
> empty of meaning like a magician's illusion.
> Having nothing to do with good or bad—right or
> wrong, one may well burst out in laughter.'

If only a small percentage of the words in this book are close to how our reality is created, then the connotations are enormous.

Imagine swimming in a Sea of Consciousness where each part is affecting all other parts. It is easy to see how information is spread, also sickness and disease. If we are all picking up information all the time, everything is available to us in this Sea of Consciousness. Yet we fail to recognise this is happening, and because of the collective conditioning, we believe the information (disease) to be ours—then by association it becomes ours.

How does information in this Sea of Consciousness get so strong that it dominates our perceptions and we believe it to be real? Simple, by the amount of energy that is put into the sea; the more energy put in, the more people subscribing to any particular belief or health issue, the more likely it is that we will be affected.

The more I understand, the less I truly know.

If any of what I have written so far is close to being the truth, then my reality is a product of where my focus has gone in the past, to what I have given my attention. I see this all around me, not just my attention but everyone's.

Our creative ability is truly amazing. It is a shame that many spend that potential creating conflict. Or is it ? Is this experience like the sandbox, a place where charge is worked out? Working out charge can appear as positive or negative, beneficial or detrimental, it all depends upon the points of view of the observer.

To Summarise the Death-Less State

I have written about my understanding of the Buddhist term 'Bardo' being a Realm of Becoming. A place of infinite possibilities. It has been said by some that this world we inhabit now is a Bardo. A Bardo may also be seen as an evolutionary step towards something other than that which we are capable of understanding from our current perspective, the limitations imposed upon as being in a physical body.

While we are 'alive' in this body, I have spoken often in this book about the Holoverse as an explanation of how our perceived reality is created. Simply said, what we put in we get back. Although the time lag between putting in and getting back has been long enough that we may well have forgotten what we put in in the first place. So when it comes back, we fail to recognise that we ordered this reality.

More likely is that whatever it was we put into the Holoverse arose from our subconscious conditioning—so something that we were not conscious of ordering. This applies to most of us as we travel through this life while still being affected by those Shadow aspects of self, the parts, according to Jung, that we have not yet fully accepted or brought into the light of consciousness. While we remain unaware of that which we put into this Cosmic Soup, aka the Holoverse, or The Mind or God, we remain victims to our past conditioning.

Imagine then that this process, or Bardo State, continues after the death of the physical body. The main difference being that there is no time lag between the thought, or emotional impulse; the manifestation of the thought or emotional impulse is immediate.

If we can recognise that all the time we are victims to our subconscious conditioning we remain unaware of that which we feed into the Soup. This does not seem to change after death of the body. There is a part of us that continues to identify with the body, the thoughts and feelings. So strongly are we attached to this, in Buddhist terms, 'body consciousness', that the attachment continues after death. The principal charge, this association with the body, that remains when we die is that which forms the Bardo State into which we put energy thus manifesting an ongoing reality.

It may be explained this way: Imagine you are in a dark place, no sense of up or down, left or right. No good or bad, right or wrong. Just an empty peaceful, quiet place. Then try to imagine an unfulfilled desire or need. See this as an energetic impulse, either a thought or an emotional charge. This thought or emotion is a transmission left over from the time you had a body which you so strongly identified with.

No different to when you were alive in the body. This is a charge that is put into the Holoverse and that will come back to you, without any judgement, no blame, just returning to you that which you put in, thus creating your perceived reality. Nothing has changed after the body dies. Only while we were in the body, there was some choice, admittedly not much of a choice because of the ongoing identification with the body, thoughts and feelings.

After the body dies, there is no longer anything about us that is able to discriminate good from bad, right from wrong (according to our perceptions). We are then simply the result of desires, thoughts, feelings that immediately create a reality, with no opportunity to change that.

The pebbles, the thoughts and emotions, that go into the pond create the world we appear to live in.

So this dark, empty place may well be an expression of the True Nature of Mind, something that we lose, according to Buddhist teachings, when we are born. We literally forget about our connection to this True Nature of Mind as we are educated into the separation of being back once more in a body.

This empty, formless place, a place of infinite possibilities, may well be the place from which all else arises. As energy, thought, emotion is put into this empty place, so it manifests immediately creating a Bardo. A state of becoming. While we remain unconscious of that which we put into this place of infinite possibilities, we will remain locked into one drama or another, without any control of what and where we 'find' ourselves.

When the body dies, so does any aspect of us that has the power to be objective about that which follows. There is no 'one' left to discern right from wrong, good from bad. This power of discrimination comes with a body. No body, no one left to discriminate. Just any residual charge that still needs to be expressed. But the association we had, may still have, with the body creates a phantom body through which we experience the Bardo State.

If the goal is to rest in the True Nature of Mind, to be at least conscious of that which we put into this Mind, then first we must let go, or understand the Shadow aspects of the self.

To me, any Shadow aspect, or even Karmic influences, aka 'charge', is dependant upon any lingering association/attachment we have to the physical body. Once the Shadow has been fully embraced and consciousness understood, once we see behind the curtain, there can be no Karma, no more subconscious charge, for these aspects are simply the product of the identification with the body. There is no more a victim to the past. Instead what remains is a conscious being able to discern what they put into the Holoverse.

Any association with the consciousness of the body slowly evaporates as we are no longer victims to any subconscious patterning to the same old degree. When we are no longer driven by any Shadow aspects, we begin to rest, more at peace with the reality we are now creating. No longer one based on conflict, or personal needs, for that which we put into the Holoverse no longer contains aspects of conflict, fear or limited personal preferences. When we no longer put these aspects into the True Nature of Mind, then we no longer get them back. When we do not get them back, there is nothing to 'do' about the parts of the manifesting reality.

Any problems that we experienced before cease to manifest because we are no longer giving any energy to that which created them in the first place. And so we become more conscious of that which we put into the Soup. Nothing changes after death of the body. Because of the steps we have taken along the way, while in a body, the realities that we face change; the energy that drives us reduces in intensity, giving us moments to reflect on that which we put into the Soup.

The less charge that still exists within us when the body dies, a very different Bardo State will arise. When there is no longer any association with the body or any desire of more, there can be no charge fed into the True Nature of Mind. Then we can rest in that state and perhaps experience an evolution of the soul.

This is the Death-Less State.

These are my thoughts, my understandings, and should be seen as such. They are not the final word. They do not claim to be the truth, just perceptions as I go through the many changes that this path brings.

I am sure there are still changes to be gone through. Patience and practice are the key to change. Stick with the old and remain in the past. Let go of the past and step into a new future. Not a future born out of any revolution, but a fire in the heart that has burnt away the old conditioned ways of being.

Once the door is open, it can never be fully closed again.

About the Author

Eric Dowsett has been following and developing the path of 'Clearing' since 1990.

During this time he has taught all over the world, sharing his understandings of this way of being.

'Clearing' can be likened to the Buddhist practice of Acceptance. By following this teaching, his understanding of the place we all have in this world has changed dramatically, not only benefitting him but all those he comes into contact with.

As his practice developed judgments fell away to be replaced with greater compassion. This has become a powerful tool to help restore more balance into the lives of individuals and the environment.

The journey is ongoing, this work is a review of his current understandings of the Buddhist 'Search for the Deathless-State'.

Eric is the author of *Collapsing the Wave*, *The Moment That Matters*, *Loving Who Shows Up*, and *First Aid: A Guide to Greater Health and Happiness*.

Learn more about Eric and clearing at:
www.ericdowsett.com